"I am thrilled ab ing book from Bart Millar *not* set us free, but being set free by the truth is real: it's going to be exciting to see how God uses *The Hurt & The Healer* in so many people's lives. I can't wait to watch it happen!"

—**Amy Grant,** Grammy Award–winning songwriter and recording artist

"I won the Winston Cup Championship in 2000, but the next day was one of the loneliest of my life. First disappointment, then anger, and eventually depression. You name it, I've experienced it. I was excited to read this book, because there's so much here that I want to grasp. What Bart and Andrew have written will help you discover your real purpose in the midst of this broken world we all live in."

—**Bobby Labonte,** professional NASCAR driver

"*The Hurt & The Healer* taught me all over again what I thought I already knew: that wholeness, contentment, and joy come not through what we do for God but through what he does for us. Take a journey into the real grace of God—not grace for those who are good enough but the grace for those of us who aren't. As Millard and Farley beautifully reveal, we are the people the Great Physician has come to heal."

—**David Gregory,** *New York Times* bestselling author of *Dinner with a Perfect Stranger*

"In a crowded arena, we stood stunned, listening to Bart Millard passionately share the original Good News. Instead of telling his listeners to be better, try harder, and care more, he is now telling them who they are in Christ. It's amazing to watch his transformation. He is now convinced that Christ in Bart is enough, and he is convincing entire audiences that Christ in them is absolutely enough! Bart wrote this book with our friend Andrew Farley, a vitally winsome and profound communicator in the movement of restoring the liberating truths of grace. Together they are giving us a wonderfully accessible open door into the healing that frees us and gives us a life worth living."

—**John Lynch, Bruce McNicol, and Bill Thrall,**
authors of *The Cure*

"I'm personally sold out to the message Bart and Andrew share in *The Hurt & The Healer*. I once saw the gospel as restrictive, and I was far from victorious. Now I see the same gospel with a whole different mindset, and the Christian life actually makes sense. In this book, Bart and Andrew show us the doorway to an abundant life and genuine healing. It's amazing to have walked through that door and to see these truths playing out in their lives and my own!"

—**Rusty Kennedy,** director of Leavener crisis
intervention and disaster relief ministry

THE HURT & THE HEALER

THE HURT & THE HEALER

Bart MILLARD   Andrew FARLEY

BakerBooks
a division of Baker Publishing Group
Grand Rapids, Michigan

Published by Baker Books
a division of Baker Publishing Group
P.O. Box 6287, Grand Rapids, MI 49516-6287
www.bakerbooks.com

Printed in the United States of America

Library of Congress Cataloging-in-Publication Data is on file at the Library of Congress, Washington, DC.

ISBN 978-0-8010-1562-5

Italics in Scripture reflect the authors' emphasis.

Published in association with the literary agency of Alive Communications, Inc., 7680 Goddard Street, Suite 200, Colorado Springs, CO 80920, alivecommunications.com.

In keeping with biblical principles of creation stewardship, Baker Publishing Group advocates the responsible use of our natural resources. As a member of the Green Press Initiative, our company uses recycled paper when possible. The text paper of this book is composed in part of post-consumer waste.

13 14 15 16 17 18 19 7 6 5 4 3 2 1

CONTENTS

"THE HURT & THE HEALER"

Lyrics by MercyMe

Why?
The question that is never far away
But healing doesn't come from the explained
Jesus, please don't let this go in vain
You're all I have, all that remains

So here I am
What's left of me
Where glory meets my suffering

I'm alive
Even though a part of me has died
I fall into Your arms open wide

You take my heart and breathe it back to life
When the hurt and the Healer collide

Breathe
Sometimes I feel it's all that I can do
Pain so deep that I can hardly move
Just keep my eyes completely fixed on You
Lord, take hold and pull me through

It's the moment when humanity
Is overcome by majesty

When grace is ushered in for good
And all our scars are understood

When mercy takes its rightful place
And all these questions fade away

When out of weakness we must bow
And hear You say, "It's over now!"

I'm alive

Jesus, come and break my fear
Wake my heart, take my tears
And find Your glory even here

INTERVIEW WITH THE AUTHORS

Tell us a little about yourselves.

Bart: My name is Bart Millard. I'm the lead singer of the band MercyMe. We recently released an album titled *The Hurt & The Healer*, and God has put a message on our hearts that we want to get out to people.

Andrew: I'm Andrew Farley. I've written several Christian books—*The Naked Gospel*, *God without Religion*, and *Heaven Is Now*. I also serve as the teaching pastor at Ecclesia: Church without Religion, a nondenominational Bible church in West Texas.

How did you each get started with what you are doing today?

Bart: MercyMe started back in 1994. We were independent until about 1999. Then we signed a record deal, and we've released a number of records since then. For whatever reason, we've seen some success in the music industry. And for whatever reason, God has given us a voice and an opportunity, almost twenty years later, to still be making music that people want to hear. We've been really blessed. If you had told me twenty years ago that this was going to happen, I would have thought you were crazy.

Andrew: In 2008, I wrote a book called *The Naked Gospel*. I prayed for about a year that it might be published, although I thought my chances were slim. But a year later, it was published, and God has been using it in so many people's lives since then. I get emails nearly every day that bring me to tears. People tell me how they found themselves begging God for answers, just like I was. Through the book, the gospel comes to mean more to them than ever before. God reaches them on a deeper level.

How did the two of you meet?

Bart: We technically met through Twitter. I personally and MercyMe as a band were going through a difficult season in our lives and our ministry. Less than a year ago, we found ourselves literally questioning why we were doing what we were doing, after eighteen years.

I grew up in church, and I would sit there singing the songs, and people would get up and say stuff like, "This is worth dying for." I felt like I was the odd man out, because I did not feel that way.

I came to Christ when I was thirteen years old, but after that initial start, I felt like something was missing. I didn't know what, but I felt like I was the only one who felt that way. But instead of asking questions, I started making a pretty good career out of just giving the answers that people wanted. The bottom line was that after eighteen years, millions of records sold, and supposedly having all the answers, it still wasn't something worth dying for.

Then a dear friend of mine, our youth pastor at our first church camp eighteen years ago, felt led to go out on the road with us for a weekend. During that weekend, he shared with us that his life had been changed. The whole truth of God's grace had come to life for him—the idea that it is not about us being bad people who should try to be good. Instead it's about knowing who we are as redeemed new creations.

Everything in my friend's life had been turned upside down. Grace changed his world, and the first person he told was me. He said, "Man, this is life-changing!" He also said, "This is now worth dying for." That really got my attention. Then he explained the whole idea of living under grace and our identity in Christ.

It's the idea that when God looks at us, no matter what we've done, no matter what we're going through, or even if we're going to do the most horrendous thing tomorrow, he already stands over it and says, "You are forgiven. You are redeemed." That's the finished work of the cross. It's not something that we wait for or hope for someday when we cross the "finish line." We are completely equipped, and we are new creations right now. All the rules have changed.

I was intrigued by everything my friend shared. Then he told me, "You need to read *The Naked Gospel*. That is a blueprint for what I'm saying." So I grabbed the book right before we were leaving for Australia. I read it on the flight over there, and I was just blown away. What blew me away was the simplicity of it. It changed everything for me. It made me think, "If this is true, if this is who Christ really is, then yes, it's worth dying for!"

I began to see that the "gap of sin" that I thought continually separated me from Christ was something that I'd been told my entire life, but it wasn't the truth.

It's more like Christ is standing right next to me the whole time, looking at sin, saying, "This really stinks, but let's get through this together, because I love you that much." That's very different from him standing on the other side saying, "You've got to find a way to get over here to me." All of a sudden, that Christ is worth dying for.

So as I read *The Naked Gospel*, I flipped out and starting tweeting about it. Andrew responded, saying he appreciated me sharing about the book. I said to him, "No, you don't understand. Either this has opened up something that is going to make me a much better minister, or I'm about to screw everything up. I'm not sure which!" That's when we first started talking about working on this book together, and that's how we first met.

Andrew: The song "The Hurt & The Healer" was written while Bart was wrestling with these things. When I looked at the lyrics of the song, I thought, I can really relate. This song resonates with me.

Much of my particular hurt early in life was a religious flavor of hurt, from growing up under legalism. But what I like about our book and the MercyMe song is that they really address *any* flavor of pain. And this Earth has plenty to throw our way.

Bart and I have a lot in common. We're roughly the same age. We both lost our fathers pretty early. We are both acquainted with loss. And I feel like we have connected with regard to our upbringing and the way that we have come to the truth. There's just something incredible about how the song and the message in the book have come together.

So why write a book together?

Bart: MercyMe was in the middle of making the record when I was introduced to *The Naked Gospel*, so it has played a huge role. In one sentence, *The Hurt & The Healer* album is about the idea that our identity is not our shame. Of course, the enemy would convince us otherwise, and we are such a performance-based society that it's hard to understand that's not who we are. That's where the album comes from.

But at a concert, I'm playing a bunch of songs, and then maybe for five or ten minutes here or there, I explain where I'm coming from. But it's very frustrating, because I'm not really a preacher. With everything going through my mind, trying to get it all out in five-minute segments is nearly impossible. Still, I am just so amped up about this message. It's something that people need to hear!

It was definitely a God thing that all of a sudden Andrew and I got in touch with each other. Not only that, but Andrew brought up the idea: "What if we did take it a step further? What if we did something to complement the record? What if you had a chance to really explain what's taken place in your life?"

Bart, how do you think the message of grace will shape your music?

Bart: The amazing thing is that there were songs I wrote over the years that I would now call "wishful thinking." In other words, they were what I hoped God was like. I'm talking about songs like "Beautiful" and "Bring the Rain." Those songs were not written from the standpoint of me having it all together. Those songs were more like, "This is what I hope you are, God, because that would be worth dying for!"

Then, when Andrew came along, explaining that God *is* this good and backing it up with Scripture, especially from the book of Hebrews, I started thinking, "This *is* who God is!" And if it can happen to me that after twenty years of being in ministry and supposedly having it together, all of a sudden the light turns on, then I just feel like a lot of people who are bound by this can be set free to find real healing.

You talk a lot about identity in the book. How do you think our past sometimes shapes our view of ourselves?

Bart: Andrew came from a more legalistic background and talks about that in his books. I came from a broken home where my identity was that I was never enough for my parents. The sad part is that a legalistic church community rescued me out of that pain, but then I just fell into another fragile identity.

I began to find identity through church. I was good at it—good at church. And I just became better and better at it. I became very good at pleasing God. But simply *trusting* him was very foreign to me.

I'm forty years old, and this is still such a new concept to me—what we call "resting in the finished work of the cross." The hardest thing for us to do is to rest, to just stop and believe that somebody else bigger than us is in control. It's a hard thing to swallow.

Our hope is that this little book becomes the beginning of a journey for a lot of people. For the first time in my life, I have a message that I think is imperative for people to hear. It has taken on a life of its own for me personally. After a ton of songs and a ton of shows, all of a sudden, it feels like I'm just now starting.

part one

THE HURT AND THE HEALER

CHAPTER 1

Guilt. Loneliness. A broken home. A broken heart. We all hurt.

Our hurts may be big or small. Whether it's physical illness or abuse, job loss or an absentee parent, poverty or imprisonment, or fear of an unknown future, pain hits all of us in one way or another.

We need healing. Our only trouble is that we don't know *where* or *how* to find it. Sometimes even our friends can't seem to help.

We might think there is something wrong with us. Maybe we are the only ones to feel such unresolved hurt. We have trouble just getting through life, making it all work.

We develop coping mechanisms to avoid more pain and to protect ourselves. Maybe things will get better with time, we tell ourselves. Maybe a bit of positive thinking will make it all go away. Maybe we just need to redouble our efforts, expend more energy, and somehow strengthen ourselves.

Some of our friends seem to be living a blissful life of blessing, getting their prayers answered, even experiencing "miracles" of one type or another. We start to feel like maybe we're the black sheep in God's family.

To make matters worse, we are ashamed that we hurt. We wish that we were stronger. We might think God is disappointed in us for hurting or that he doesn't care. We would never say it out loud, but we might even think God is the one kicking us when we're down. Maybe we believe we deserve to hurt because of all the things we've done wrong, and God is just rubbing it in as he teaches us a lesson.

But that's not who God really is. No, God is our Counselor, our Comforter, our Healer. He's not shocked or disappointed with us when we hurt. We can be open and honest with him. We don't have to pretend. He wants us to be transparent about our pain. That's the only way real healing can take place in our lives. And, yes, that means being honest about *all* the feelings we have, not just the positive or spiritual-looking ones.

As we lean on God the Healer, we hear the gentle voice of his Spirit teaching us how we have tried to get our needs met in ways that only bring disappointment. And he reveals how we can get our needs met like never before.

The Ancient Story

At our core, we have the need to be fully *accepted* and to enjoy a rich, meaningful *purpose* in life. At one time, we the human race had all of our needs met. Adam and Eve were designed in God's image. They were full, complete, lacking nothing—perfect in every way. But then they bought the lie that they needed *more*.

Satan convinced them that they should go shopping for their own form of morality and ethics, outside of God. The result? The presence of God's life within them was lost. Their connection with him was no more. Their fullness was gone. Their needs were no longer met. Instead, they turned to a system of trying to do good and avoid evil in order to regain that feeling of perfection.

They measured themselves. They fell short of their own self-imposed standard. They were ashamed. Then God came to them and essentially asked, "Who told you there was something wrong with you? By what standard are you judging yourselves? Why are you ashamed?" (see Gen. 3:11).

From that day forward, we the human race became *achievers*. We now seek to achieve to a standard that will ensure we feel accepted by those around us. We crave approval. We want someone to tell us that we are okay. We buy the lie that our value comes from what those around us say or think about us. If they feel okay about us, then we feel okay too. We hop on the performance treadmill, and we "do" in order to "be."

The Table Turner

Jesus Christ came to change all of this. He lived a perfect life, meeting all standards and then some, in our place. He died on the cross as full payment for all of our sins. God is fully satisfied with his payment, and through Jesus Christ we meet a perfect standard. He credits it to our account. Our spiritual connection with God is regained. The spiritual life once lost in the Garden is restored.

Do we believe Jesus Christ is the Son of God? Do we believe he died and rose again? Do we believe he made full payment for our sins? Have we opened the door of our life to him, allowing him to initiate real change from within? These are the most basic questions to consider if we want *spiritual* healing.

Any genuine change starts with Jesus. He responds when we call on his name and invite him to heal us:

> Jesus Christ, I believe you are the Son of God. I believe you died as full payment for my sins. I believe you rose from the dead to offer me a new, eternal life. I open the door of my life. I ask you to come and live within me. Make me new, a child of God, and show me how to find healing in you from this day forward.

Simple faith in Jesus Christ brings us an eternal, spiritual healing. And spiritual healing *is* a big deal. It means that we receive forgiveness for all of our sins. It means we become God's children, holy and blameless.

Still, there is so much more.

God the Healer can even bring *emotional* healing into our lives. He is calling us to compare our current belief system with what he says is really true about us. And he knows us better than anyone else.

> *Who am I?*
> *What am I like, spiritually, on the inside?*
> *How can I find real fulfillment?*
> *What do I do with all the anger, fear, and pain inside me?*

Reliable answers to these questions can only come from the Healer himself. This book is designed to help you put together the pieces you need to understand exactly *how* God can be the Healer of your many hurts.

Questions to Consider

- What have been some of the biggest hurts in your life?
- Can you identify the ways you try to deal with pain? How well have these strategies worked?
- Consider taking a moment to pray and ask God to use this book to bring you authentic, enduring healing in the areas you need it most.

Talking to Jesus

Jesus, thank you that I can be transparent with you about my deepest hurts. You encourage me to be open about my weaknesses and struggles, making my requests known to you. I look to you as my Counselor and Comforter. I believe you can heal me. Amen.

CHAPTER 2

If you hurt, you are not alone.

The world we live in might have us believe that any sort of so-called negative feelings we experience are highly unusual. We are supposedly abnormal, out of the ordinary. We need those feelings fixed, fast, we might think. Everyone else seems to be coping with life just fine.

Don't believe the lie. God's Word speaks to our guilt, our anxiety, and our fear, because the Healer is well aware that we *can* and *will* experience these! Everyone encounters trouble of some kind.

We all live on planet Earth.

A Prime Example

Consider the apostle Paul, the author of many letters to the early church. Paul was imprisoned, beaten with rods, stoned, shipwrecked, robbed, slandered, hungry, thirsty, cold, and homeless throughout his life (2 Cor. 11:23–27). Such a godly man encountered this sort of trouble and pain?

We all meet difficulty in this life, no matter who we are. The key is how we *respond* to it. The apostle Paul discovered that by admitting his frailty, not denying it, he opened the door for God's healing power (2 Cor. 12:9–10). But weakness is not something we want to own up to. When trouble hits, we try to be strong, capable, and adequate to the task. Unexpectedly, though, it is only when we are transparent about our trouble and honest about our weakness that we find true healing and strength.

So don't buy the idea that you are abnormal or a special case because you hurt. Your feelings may be all over the place, but God created us to experience emotions. Riding the roller coaster of our emotions is a *normal* human experience. None of us can set out to change our feelings and expect any real success.

No, the answer lies elsewhere.

Brainless Reactors

Some of us cannot wait for the release of the next big horror flick. We wait in line all day for it, and finally, after hours of waiting, we take our seat in the theater. Shortly thereafter, images flash before our eyes, and our hearts start pounding. When frightened, our bodies even tense up. We grab the armrest. Some of us might even let out a bloodcurdling scream! Of course, the whole time, we sit safely in the movie theater, facing no real danger of any kind.

Our emotions are brainless reactors. Emotions make no distinction between a present reality and a fictitious fantasy. Emotions cannot think for themselves. They merely respond.

We might presume that our emotions are wild, all over the place, and unpredictable. But they're not. Actually, our emotions are consistently and predictably a product of our thinking.

We feel what we think.

Input and Output

In the world of computing, programmers talk about *input* and *output*. They enter data into computers—that's called the *input*. Then the computer processes that data and produces some sort of results—that's called the *output*. There are many kinds of output. Output might be displayed on a computer monitor, or printed on a sheet of paper, or even heard as music.

One thing is for sure: without any input going in, there won't be any output going out. And the *type* of input determines the type of output:

input → COMPUTER → output

Our minds operate much like a computer. They need input to produce output. The input is the thoughts we choose to entertain, while the output is the feelings that result. Again, with certain thoughts going in, there can only be certain feelings going out:

thoughts → MIND → feelings

We think. Then we feel. But if we don't understand this natural order, we might panic when we experience unwanted feelings. The natural result is that we try to shove down our feelings, to rid ourselves of them, or to put a Band-Aid over them somehow.

thoughts → MIND → feelings
↑
we try to "fix"

We look to hide or change our feelings rather than realizing *it is our thinking that needs to change*. Try as we may, we cannot control or change our emotions. That approach will never, ever work. We can only change what we choose to think, not what we feel.

God's Word never forbids us to *feel* something. Take anger, for example. The Bible never once says to not feel angry. Instead, it says, "Be angry and do not sin" (Eph. 4:26 ESV). This means that it is okay to feel anger, but we shouldn't *act* on those angry feelings with cruel or destructive behavior. This is very different from telling us not to feel anger at all. That would be impossible!

We were designed by God to feel all kinds of things. We cannot eliminate certain emotions. We can only *choose which thoughts* we allow to drive them.

Belief Systems: Our "Biggest" Thoughts

"No, you don't understand. My emotions are totally wacko! I feel like a real basket case sometimes, consumed with worry and fear. And when it's not those things, it's guilt. Clearly, my problem is *emotional*."

It certainly may be that your emotions seem "wacko" to you right now. But we assure you—the root of the problem is the thoughts driving those emotions. Your emotions are actually healthy in the sense that they are doing what emotions do—they *react*. So it is the thoughts that we allow ourselves to dwell on that may be "wacko" or unhealthy. This is why our thought life must be addressed for real healing to occur.

When we find ourselves experiencing the ups and downs of emotion, we can know that those feelings are not birthed out of thin air. They stem from our thinking. And where do our thoughts come from? Many of our thoughts are motivated by our larger, overarching *belief systems*. The belief systems we have about ourselves and about God determine many of our everyday thoughts, which then dictate our emotions.

Jesus is our Healer. In his Word, the Healer does not appeal to our emotions in order to change them. Instead, he appeals to our minds in order to renew them (Rom. 12:2). As we experience the renewing of our *mindsets*, we can walk through trouble without the trouble itself determining how we *think* and consequently *feel* about ourselves. The trouble may not go away for some time, but our attitudes and responses in the midst of circumstances can change dramatically. As the Healer renews our minds, we can experience significant change in how we feel.

Questions to Consider

- In what ways have you been tempted to act strong, capable, and adequate within yourself? What emotions might you have suppressed in the process?

- Some approaches to healing attempt to change or "fix" our feelings. How is God's renewing of our minds different?
- Had you ever considered how directly your thoughts lead to your feelings? What sort of thoughts do you think the Healer might want to renew within you?

Talking to Jesus

Thank you, Jesus, that I don't have to stuff down or hide my feelings from you. You created me to think and to feel. Remind me not to try to "fix" my unwanted feelings but instead to allow you to show me the thoughts that bring them on. Heal my broken belief systems as you renew my mind by your Spirit and your Word. I am open, Jesus, to your truth that sets me free. Teach me your ways so that I might think new thoughts, your thoughts, even in my life's most difficult moments. Amen.

CHAPTER 3

Recently, a New Zealand man was informed by doctors that he had developed a terminal form of cancer. You can imagine what he might have felt upon receiving the news: shock and a sense of urgency.

The man and his wife sold their home and spent their entire life's savings to fulfill their "bucket list" of things they wanted to do together before he died.

Shortly thereafter, doctors came back with news of a misdiagnosis. Apparently, the man was not dying from cancer after all! He could expect to live a long, normal life. Now, imagine the feelings that set in after he received *that* news. He probably felt confused, then relieved.

After getting the initial diagnosis of cancer, the man experienced a host of overwhelming emotions. Those feelings likely drove him to make some radical decisions. Notice the process we humans tend to go through:

we think → we feel → we choose

Once the misdiagnosis was revealed, this process started all over again for the man. New thoughts brought new feelings and new choices. In both cases, thoughts were the driving force. It made no difference whether those thoughts were based on *truth* or *error*. Each time, with the original diagnosis and with the revelation of the misdiagnosis, the mind took in information that led to all kinds of emotions. These thoughts and feelings then led to choices.

Switch the Order

We humans tend to think first, then feel, then choose. While this is very common, it is not what God wants for us as we live by faith in Jesus Christ. Instead, the Healer would have us *think*, then *choose*, then *feel* what we may. This is what it means to walk by faith, not by sight or feeling.

We can choose apart from our feelings. We can even choose *against* our feelings when they cry out in contradiction to what we know is God's truth about us. While the world might tell us that only hypocrites choose to live contrary to what they feel, that is far from God's view. Many times, God *wants* us to choose contrary to our misleading emotions. As we walk by faith, the Healer's divine order for us is the following:

we set our minds → we choose → we feel

We shouldn't wait to *feel* that something is true before we *choose* to walk by it. Our emotions may or may not ever line up perfectly with the Healer's truth about us. Nevertheless, we can discard error and choose to walk by truth in the moment. And it is truth, not emotion, that sets us free to experience God's healing in our lives.

There is a doorway to our mind, and there is a doorknob on the door. We choose what we let through the doorway. The Healer wants us to know that we can take any thought captive, making it submissive to Jesus and his healing truth about us (2 Cor. 10:5).

Choose Healing

To find real healing, we have to make *choices*. Frankly, not everyone seems to make those choices. If we are not careful, our thought lives can lead us down the road toward depression or, for some, even toward suicidal thoughts.

We might spiral into such a self-focus, inundated with fearful and hopeless thoughts. Then when our emotions follow suit, we conclude that something is wrong with us. We have a "condition," we might think. Perhaps we even take on a new identity rooted in our struggle. We categorize and label ourselves, believing that there is something unusual and wrong with our emotions.

All the while, the reality is that our depressed feelings are simply responding to the depressing thoughts that we feed our mind. Remember input and output—what goes in must come out! So as depressing thoughts go into the computer of our mind, then depressed feelings come out. It's a simple equation. And there is a straightforward solution—what the Healer calls the renewing of our minds (Rom. 12:2).

We've already seen that emotions aren't good or bad, or right or wrong. They are simply indicators of the thoughts that fill our minds and the belief systems that produce those thoughts. So go ahead, let yourself feel, and talk to God about all those feelings. But if you're hoping for the healing of your emotions, don't try to stuff them down or "fix" them. Instead, look to the source—your thought life. God tells us that we will only be transformed by the renewing of our minds (Rom. 12:2).

Consider asking the Healer: "What error am I setting my mind on that brings me such fear, guilt, or pain? What is your truth in this situation that will set me free?" Destructive emotions will only change as we search our belief systems to see where they do and do not line up with the truth of God's healing grace. Just as error binds us and brings on destructive feelings, God's truth sets us free and brings on emotional healing.

Choose Your Channel

Consider the FM/AM radio. The FM signal carries more information, providing higher resolution, finer quality audio. Conversely, the AM signal only offers lower resolution, lesser quality audio. You'll find a lot of cheap talk shows on AM.

Our minds work much like an FM/AM radio. There's an FM channel, the Father's Mentoring channel. His FM channel offers high resolution, quality messages to our mind. But there's also an AM channel, the Alternative Messages channel. This channel offers a whole lot of "cheap talk" about who we are and where we can find meaning and fulfillment.

When we listen to that alternative channel, we take in what the world has to say about how to make life work. We ultimately experience confusion and a lack of contentment.

But when we choose to listen to the Father's Mentoring channel, we find ourselves being built up into the liberating truth about who God really is and who we are as his children. We end up enjoying an intimate relationship with God, experiencing a life built on a firm foundation.

Which channel have you been listening to? If your thoughts about God and about yourself have been beating you up, isn't it time you changed the channel?

Questions to Consider

- The world subtly communicates that we should go with what we feel. But the Healer calls us to set our minds on his truth to determine our choices. Which of these two systems do you tend to operate under?

  the world's system: think → feel → choose

  God's system: set your mind → choose → feel

- God does not define us by the emotions we feel or even the thoughts we might often think. Is there any label (hothead, control freak, depressed, etc.) that you have adopted as your identity other than "holy, blameless child of God"?
- Had you ever thought about the two distinct "channels" in your thought life? Can you identify some

of the "cheap talk" you've been listening to? Are you willing to turn the channel to hear what the Father's Mentoring channel has to say about you?

Talking to Jesus

Jesus, I thank you for the natural functioning of my mind and emotions, that my feelings follow my thoughts. In the times I need it the most, remind me that I can choose apart from my feelings. Remind me that even when my feelings cry out against my choice, I can still choose based on your truth about me. Teach me who I truly am as your child, a new creation, holy and blameless before you. I want to set my mind on your truth all the days of my life. Amen.

CHAPTER 4

In February 2012, an American stuntman named Nik Wallenda became the first person in more than a hundred years to walk a tightrope across Niagara Falls. With one billion viewers glued to their televisions, Wallenda carefully placed his feet, one after another, along a two-inch-wide cable and walked across a 1,800-foot gap between the United States and Canada. After nearly thirty minutes, he made it across, receiving the applause of thousands on site. It was exciting to watch, even on television!

But when viewers examined the situation more closely, they realized that safety officials had insisted on a backup plan, just in case things went south. As Wallenda walked the tightrope, he wore a harness attached to a thin safety cable trailing inconspicuously behind him. Even if he were to fall off the tightrope, the safety cable fastened behind him to the tightrope would catch him. He'd be hanging there until someone could bring him to safety on the other side.

Life can be painful, even dangerous. But God's healing grace is *our* safety cable. God's grace enables us to move forward in life with confidence, knowing that when we fall, we find safety and security in the love of Jesus. Even in the midst of our worst performance, he never leaves us; he never forsakes us.

How God Heals

God spells healing: c-o-v-e-n-a-n-t.

A covenant is a promise, an agreement, a contract. If you've been wondering how you can know and experience God's healing touch in your life, there is no better way than through coming to understand the new covenant. God shows us what his healing grace really looks like *through the new covenant*.

The old way of the law was a long list of rules and regulations that the people of Israel had to obey. It was an all-or-nothing system under which *everyone* failed (Gal. 3:10; 5:3; James 2:10). The Israelites promised to keep up their end of the bargain (Exod. 24:7) but blew it continually. Therefore, God turned away from them, because of their inability to crank out faithfulness (Heb. 8:9–10).

So if this new covenant really is new and different, then it has to solve our faithfulness problem. It has to accomplish what the old covenant could not. And that is exactly what we find in God's new covenant—a radical, new way that centers on *God's promise to himself*!

> Because God wanted to make *the unchanging nature of his purpose* very clear to the heirs of what was promised, he confirmed it with an oath. God did this so that, *by two unchangeable things* in which it is impossible for God to lie, we who have fled to take hold of the hope set before us may be greatly encouraged. *We have this hope as an anchor for the soul, firm and secure.* (Heb. 6:17–19)

The "two unchangeable things" here are God and God. So this new way is about the trustworthy character of God, and also the trustworthy character of God. Yes, you read that one right. This new covenant is all about God and God. We are simply beneficiaries of the pact that he made with himself! This is why we are anchored to such an incredibly secure hope that can heal our hurts.

God had already seen the best efforts we humans could make. For thousands of years, he witnessed our many attempts to please him. So under this new way, God put the focus on himself and his ability, not on us and our abilities.

the new covenant promise: God ⟷ God

Where are we in this picture? We are the ones who wake up every day and simply give thanks to God for all he has done. This unshakable, unbreakable, and rock-solid promise is what brings genuine healing into our lives.

It's Not about You!

Sometimes we might wonder where we stand with God. But is our answer to that question drawn from what *we* are trying to do for him or from what Jesus has done for us? We should make sure our perspective jibes with God's new way.

Under God's new way, it's not about us.

Even when we are faithless (which happens to all of us!), he remains faithful (2 Tim. 2:13). When we make our relationship with God about us and what we are doing for him, it only brings guilt and confusion. The Healer longs for us to relax in the goodness of his grace. God wants us to realize the benefits of his own faithfulness to himself. He wants us to see it's all about his Son, Jesus. It's really *not* about us.

So what if you are as secure and loved as Jesus himself? God tells us that "love is perfected with us, so that we may have confidence in the day of judgment; because *as He is, so also are we in this world*" (1 John 4:17 NASB). God loves us with a perfect love. His love is designed to give us an earth-shattering confidence. Even right now, in this world, *we are as safe as Jesus*.

Don't let anyone tell you different.

Can it really be this good? Isn't this just some sort of cheap grace? No, it's very *expensive* grace, since it came at the price of Jesus hanging on a cross. Therefore, it has been paid for in full and given to us as a free gift. But we need to go ahead and *own it*. We are surely going to need it!

God's New Way to Healing

Have you ever noticed the effect that rules have in our lives? Rules actually make us want to break them! The Bible itself tells us this, as it reveals that the old way of commandments just *gave sin an opportunity to thrive* (Rom. 7:8).

God didn't introduce the old way to prevent sin. No, he introduced the old way so that people would realize how much sinning they were actually doing! He tells us that "the law was brought in so that the trespass might *increase*" (Rom. 5:20).

The answer has always been faith in God's grace, not a bunch of religious rules. Under a rule-based system, people automatically resort to human effort. They try their best to keep all the rules. But that's not what God wants from us! Remember, he has already seen what we humans can do under that sort of system.

Fail. Rededicate. Fail. Rededicate. Fail.

That's what it looks like for anyone under dead religion. And that's not our destiny. No, God's new way changes all of that.

What if God were willing to forgive you of everything you've ever done? What if God were willing to save you forever, sustaining your salvation for you? What if God were even willing to live through you, being your source for all good behavior? And what if all you had to do was just *let* him?

That *is* God's new way.

The new covenant is not some dead religion of rules and regulations that we have to keep. No, we don't begin our relationship with God by following a bunch of rules. We begin it by grace. So we don't continue in our relationship with God by following rules either.

We continue by that very same grace. Jesus is enough, from start to finish. So what if we just fix our eyes on him—what he has done for us and even what he is doing in and through us today? What would such a Jesus-focused life look like?

Jesus has anchored us to a real, secure hope. He has given us a new identity and purpose. As we realize how incredible this is and set our minds on it, we experience peace. This is how we start to experience healing and begin to live *from* Jesus, not merely *for* him.

Questions to Consider

- Have you been concerned about your faithfulness to God? Are you willing to shift your focus toward *his* faithfulness to you?
- First John 4:17 says, "as He is, so also are we in this world" (NASB). What does it mean to you to be as safe and secure as Jesus himself?
- A rule-based religious system just makes you want to break the rules. How is God's new covenant way different?
- Do you believe that God's kindness and grace toward you can be enough motivation for you to live uprightly? Why or why not?

Talking to Jesus

Jesus, the new covenant brings your healing touch into my life. I thank you for securing a place for me, no matter what, because of your own faithfulness to yourself. Thank you that I am as safe as you. Your new way of grace is so much better than any religious rules. You motivate me from the heart, where your desires are written within me. I choose to celebrate your incredible accomplishment on the cross and through the resurrection. I celebrate my new life in you. Thank you, Jesus. Amen.

part two

WHEN WE DON'T MEASURE UP

CHAPTER 5

Most of us today probably don't look to the Old Testament for religious rules to live by. Still, many of us may adopt another form of law, a modern-day set of rules or standards by which we live. We feel good about ourselves only when we live up to these standards, and we feel our self-worth dwindling away when we fail to meet them.

This sort of self-improvement system can seem so "spiritual." We might try to say all the right things and do all the right things to make ourselves feel like we're acceptable in our own eyes, the eyes of God, or the eyes of others. For some people, it might be church attendance. For others, it might be a personal time of Bible study. For others, it might be sharing their faith with others. Some might hold themselves to a certain standard of "niceness" or people pleasing.

When we fall short of these self-imposed standards, we are prone to believe the lie that we can only feel good about ourselves when we live up to them. If we don't attain to them, we might only find relief as we try to somehow make up for our failures.

For us (the authors), the standards took on a religious flavor. We both found ourselves driven to excel in a "self-improvement program" of our own making. We ended up living from a *have-to* mentality rather than enjoying what God intends for us—the freedom of a *want-to* relationship. Without even realizing it, we lived under a modern-day form of "law" of our own making. Here is what it looked like:

Commandment 1: Thou shalt go to church.

Commandment 2: Thou shalt read your Bible.

Commandment 3: Thou shalt share your faith.

Commandment 4: Thou shalt be a good witness.

Commandment 5: Thou shalt stay in God's will.

Of course, these all seem like good things! But the problem with adopting this modern-day "Christian law" system is that we ended up not allowing ourselves to feel right with God (and good about ourselves) unless we lived up to them. We only felt good when we had logged "enough" time in a book or in a church building. We only felt right when we were out sharing our faith or being seen as "spiritual."

This is a works righteousness. Of course, we knew this to-do list was *not* our ticket to heaven. We relied on God's grace for that. But then we would turn right around and look to our own performance for daily "status" with God. We failed to see that our daily right standing before God was entirely because of God's new covenant promise—God's promise to himself.

We were making it about ourselves, not our Savior.

Pleading for the Fifth

The fifth "commandment" on the list, trying to find and stay in God's will, is a very popular idea these days. Many of us might think we get right with God and stay right with God by choosing the things we perceive as being "his will" for our lives. But we need to remember that our rightness with God was a gift given to us in Jesus Christ. It was never about making all the "right" daily choices to get right with God.

God's will is not something that we have to go find and then somehow work to remain in. God's will is in plain sight for all of us to see. So if you've been searching for God's will for your life, here it is!

> Rejoice always; pray without ceasing; in everything give thanks; for *this is God's will for you* in Christ Jesus. (1 Thess. 5:16–18 NASB)

Celebrate the beautiful truths of the new covenant. *Give thanks* for Jesus and all he has done for you. *Talk openly* and honestly with your heavenly Dad. These things are God's will for our lives, shared plainly with us.

Essentially, *God's will is Jesus*—Jesus in us and Jesus expressed through us.

Simple, isn't it? Unfortunately, many of us miss the simplicity of God's will and even start to panic about what we need to do to get "in" his will and then stay in it. Which spouse? Which house? Which job? Which car? Finding and staying in God's will can become a full-time job—our standard to meet in order to feel good about ourselves. Just like the other four so-called Christian rules we listed, finding God's will and trying to stay in it can become another form of works righteousness.

The Only Sensible Solution

No matter what standards we may have adopted, the only sensible solution is to *drop all standards as the means to feeling good about ourselves.* This is what being "under grace" really means. We drop the standards we've adopted for measuring ourselves, and we unabashedly cling to God's full, no-holds-barred acceptance of us. We choose to agree that we are 100 percent loved and approved even if we never set foot in church again, even if we never read our Bibles ever again, even if we never share our faith with anyone ever again, and even if we fail miserably in how we treat people. While all of those activities may naturally flow from our relationship with God, his unconditional love for us is not affected by any of them!

When we live out of any sense of having to meet a standard to feel okay about ourselves, we are not really living under grace. At salvation, God made us die to law-like standards so that we can now live in the freedom of his life-healing grace (Rom. 7:4; Gal. 2:19). God wants us to honor the finished work of Jesus, claiming our full acceptance in him, resting in what he did for us. This puts a stop to all our futile attempts to "get right" and "stay right" with God. Instead, we realize that by one sacrifice we *are* right, now and forever (Heb. 10:14).

Once we agree that God's love and acceptance will never diminish, we begin to relax in his divine approval. We escape the "thou shalt" rules of our own invention and rest securely in the arms of our Healer. We see that his face is *always* toward us. Once we realize the route to wholeheartedly accepting ourselves just as God accepts us, we can turn to those around us and begin to accept them too with no strings attached. Then, as we relate to others, we no longer subtly (or not so subtly!) look down on them because they fail to meet our "standard." Instead, we discover that we ourselves are "accepted in the beloved" (Eph. 1:6 KJV) only by God's grace, not by our performance. As we soak in God's unconditional approval of us, we can exude that same attitude toward others (John 13:34; 1 John 3:23). We start living from the embrace of God's grace.

Questions to Consider

- What rules or standards have you sought to live by in order to feel good about yourself? Have you ever thought about self-improvement not being a "good" thing?
- Do you believe your relationship with God can move from a have-to mentality to a want-to mentality? What differences would that make in your life?
- Have you been trying to get "in" God's will and then stay in it? How does knowing that "God's will is Jesus in us and expressed through us" bring you freedom?

- Are you willing to believe in and rest in the Healer's unconditional approval of you? If so, take a moment to tell God that now.

Talking to Jesus

Jesus, thank you that I am dead to the law and alive to you. Thank you for freeing me from having to meet any standard in order to feel good about myself. Thank you for making me new at the core and inscribing your loving desires on the lining of my heart. The covenant you have invited me to is so liberating, not burdensome in the least! Thank you that your face is always toward me and that I am truly accepted by you, with no strings attached. Teach me to rest in your unfailing love and approval. Amen.

CHAPTER 6

We know that the Healer wants us to cast our anxiety on him and allow his peace to guard our minds. But what does that peace look like? And how exactly does it come about in our lives?

God's perfect love for us is supposed to cast away all of our fears (1 John 4:18). Still, we might shake our fist at heaven, shouting, "I want to know your love! I want to *feel* your love!" We wonder where God is and why he isn't responding.

But what if God has *already* responded to us? What if his deep love for us has already been demonstrated? What if we just haven't known where to look? The Bible tells us that God demonstrated his love for us in this: that Christ died for us (Rom. 5:8). Still, we think, what in the world does Christ dying and being resurrected two thousand years ago have to do with my quest to feel his love here and now?

We know that Jesus's death and resurrection provide a way for us to have forgiveness of our sins and a place in heaven. But it may be difficult for us to fathom how the death and resurrection of Christ can have any real, tangible effect on our present pain. There *is* something here to discover. Yes, the Healer wants to reveal to us how Jesus can be the answer to our fear, anxiety, and deepest hurts.

Acceptance: God's Cure for Anxiety

Anxiety. It hits all of us in one way or another. Anxiety occurs when we start watching that scary movie projected on the screen of our mind. In the feature film, there we are, front and center, *failing* in some way in front of our peers.

Social anxiety. Test anxiety. There are many flavors of anxiety out there. Anxiety stems from the fear of future failure. Think about it. In the times when you have felt anxious, what thoughts were attached to your anxiety? The potential for embarrassment? The potential for things not going your way? The potential for others to see you fall short in some way?

These scenarios breed anxiety.

The only real cure for these "hooks" in our thought life is *knowing our freedom to fail.* Are you willing to fail in front of others? Unless you are, you will spend your life being held captive by the fear of failure. But if we believe that we are free to fail, then the movie scene of our potential failure no longer captivates us. We don't obsess over what could happen. We realize our value and importance is not dependent on looking good in front of others. Then anxiety about future failure no longer holds a grip on us.

Of course, this doesn't mean we go out and seek failure with a martyr-like complex. It simply means that we give up our "right" to success and trust God with any and all results, no matter what they might be. *But we can only make this choice when we have an identity, a value, and a purpose that is not wrapped up in succeeding in the eyes of others.* We must get our identity and worth from Someone else altogether. This is why it is essential to know exactly how accepted we are in Jesus Christ. God's acceptance of us is based on grace, because of the work of Jesus and nothing else—at all. God's acceptance of us is his never-ending embrace of who we are. God's acceptance of us is his unconditional approval of who we are.

God's total acceptance of us is what makes us truly free to fail!

Failure and Success Don't Define Us

We can find ourselves freezing up like a deer in the headlights at the sight of a new challenge. This happens as we look to success as the basis for building identity or worth. When we fail, we engage in self-condemnation, beating ourselves up for our inability to look good and "go places." Then we take on failure as our identity. If we believe ourselves to be a poor performer, we might seek out friends who don't make us feel so inferior. Our relationships are limited as we are only willing to develop friendships with those who are compatible with our view of ourselves and our worth. Conversely, when we succeed, we may buy the lie that our identity and worth are wrapped up in those achievements. If we believe ourselves to be a good performer, then we might see little need for grace. We begin to measure others, judging whether they fit our view of "success."

The good news of the gospel breaks through this achievement-based, anxiety-ridden way of thinking. God has given us both his acceptance and his approval apart from our works. Once our value is rooted in our spiritual identity, not in our earthly accomplishments, we can more easily be open to new challenges we face. Whether we succeed or fail at them has no bearing on our purpose in this life, as our *life's purpose is to know Christ and to live from him*, regardless of what is or is not accomplished from the world's perspective. Failure or fear of failure does not need to weigh us down as we *already* have God's unconditional forgiveness and approval along the way.

Once we agree to leave behind the negative thought patterns that have trapped us in the fear of failure, we can see ourselves through God's eyes. Do you realize how he sees you? He finds you fully pleasing to himself, and he accepts you no matter what! "What, then, shall we say in response to these things? If God is for us, who can be against us?" (Rom. 8:31).

Questions to Consider

- What sort of failure scenarios do you allow to play in your mind that incite anxiety? How might understanding our freedom to fail free you from the "hook" of those scenarios?
- In what ways have you become enamored with the allure of looking good by your performance? How has this fed your anxiety at times?
- How have you allowed past failures to label you as a "failer"? How might resting in God's unconditional

acceptance and approval of you bring real change into your life?

- We all want to know and experience the love of God. But do you think we are sometimes looking in the wrong place? Where *exactly* should we look?

Talking to Jesus

Jesus, I sometimes allow myself to be overtaken by thoughts of anxiety. I project into the future with what might happen, and it paralyzes me. But I choose to release my future to you to do with it whatever you choose. I trust you, Jesus, with every ounce of it. Thank you that I am not defined by my past failures or my future failures. I am free to fail because you have secured for me an unshakable place in you. Remind me to look to you—to your death and resurrection—for the solid evidence of acceptance and approval I so desperately need to feel safe. Amen.

CHAPTER 7

You are worth Jesus!

Not only are we whole through the presence of Christ within us, but God has attributed an infinite value to us by giving us his own righteousness. He calls us "the righteousness of God" (2 Cor. 5:21).

This means that we are worth Jesus.

Imagine a set of scales with two trays, one on each side, hanging by chains. Jesus is on one side of the scale, and you are on the other side. You and Jesus weigh the same to God. You carry the same value.

You are the righteousness of God. It is *not* that God is pretending you are valuable to him. No, he has actually made you valuable at the core. And he has determined that you are infinitely valuable to him, forever.

We desperately need a deep sense of value as a person in order to function mentally and emotionally in the way that God intends. Having a sense of irrevocable value can and will affect our attitudes and actions.

If we merely try to change our behavior without realizing that it is our quest for value that is motivating much of what we do, then we engage in a fruitless endeavor. We might spend our entire lives hunting for love and acceptance from the people around us, but the hole at the center of our being can only be filled by the Healer himself. He designed us in such a way that we need him housed within us to be made whole.

Regeneration: *Really* Righteous

God has done more than credit righteousness to our spiritual bank account. He has actually brought real change to our human spirit, the core of our being. His Spirit has come to live in us, and he has literally and actually made us new and righteous on the inside.

We have undergone *a change of nature*. This is very different from God simply calling us righteous or looking at us "as if" we were righteous. It is a new birth, a regeneration, a DNA swap, a heart surgery, a literal transformation as we have been born of God's Spirit (John 3:6; 1 John 5:4).

Once we see who we really are on the inside, at the core, we realize that we don't need to *become* someone anymore. We don't need to become what other people want us to be. Instead, we can wake up every day and *be ourselves*. Being who we are is enough. In Jesus Christ, we now have an adequacy that we should be aware of: "not that we are adequate in ourselves . . . but *our adequacy is from God*" (2 Cor. 3:5 NASB). We are complete in Christ, not lacking any spiritual equipping in him (Eph. 1:3; Col. 2:10). We don't have to go shopping for more of Jesus or more of what the world might tell us we need in order to be "okay."

You Are *in* Christ

God says we are who we are by birth, *not* by what we do. We are born *in* Adam. That is our original identity. Then, at salvation, we are crucified with Christ and reborn *in* him. This is our new identity. We are who we are by spiritual death and rebirth (Rom. 6:6; Gal. 2:20), by whom we are now *in*. Our new spiritual location *in Christ* is what gives us a new nature and an irrevocable identity as children of God.

Still, we may have accepted a lesser identity for ourselves. If we grew up being told by our parents that we were never good enough, never smart enough, never attractive enough, never quite acceptable to them, we inevitably absorbed this view of ourselves. Then we began to measure and reject ourselves much like our parents did. Consequently, we might now be thinking and acting like who *they* said we are.

Our sense of identity and worth needs to come from what God says about us, not from what we have accomplished (or *not* accomplished!) and not from what others might say about us, whether good or bad.

And here's another reality check for us: when we base our identity on what others think of us, we are actually basing it on what *we think they think of us*. Behind closed doors, it may be an altogether different story! That's just the way gossip and rumors on planet Earth really work.

Even if people think highly of us, that can and does change with time. The ups and downs of vacillating opinion eventually exhaust us. If we base our identity and worth on the assessments of those around us, no matter who they are, we will ride the roller coaster of human opinion and always be insecure along the ride.

We are meant for something a whole lot more stable. We are designed to base our identity and self-worth on something unchangeable—the unconditional, unwavering opinion of our heavenly Father.

We can never do anything to change his approval of who we are. Nothing. There is not any sin imaginable that we can commit that would alter how he feels about us. Wow! This is an identity that brings unshakable value to our lives. When we align our thoughts about ourselves with God's thoughts about us, then and only then will we have a *proper* self-image. All the false identities, the fragile ones that eventually come crashing down, fade away in our minds as we embrace the indestructible, eternal identity given to us by the Healer himself.

You Are a Member of Christ's Body

We may have sought a sense of belonging by joining a fraternity, a sorority, or some other social group or organization. Of course, there is nothing wrong with joining groups like these. But they inevitably disappoint and fail us if we are even subconsciously looking to them as a substitute for our place, our role, in the body of Christ.

When we join a group or organization, we sometimes need to pay an entrance fee or perform a rite of passage in order to gain acceptance into the group. When it comes to being a member of the body of Christ, Jesus himself paid the entrance fee. The rite of passage was carried out on the cross and through the resurrection.

When we accept Jesus Christ's payment for our sins and his gift of new life, we freely receive membership as part of his body. If we then go out and frantically chase after acceptance elsewhere, we essentially place more importance on *their* approval than on our membership in Christ's body.

Part of our new identity in Christ is that *we belong to something much larger than ourselves*. We are each members of the body of Christ on planet Earth. This can bring us a deep sense of belonging.

God has seated us at his table and given us a position of honor. He has allowed us to participate in his divine nature (2 Pet. 1:4) and express his love to the world around us. We are part of something huge and historical. God is building his kingdom, and we are royalty within it (1 Pet. 2:9)!

Questions to Consider

- We are now *in* Christ and *complete* in him. How might this truth affect the way you view yourself and your pursuits in life?
- What does it mean to you to have died with Christ and to be reborn of God's Spirit?
- What does it mean to you to be "worth Jesus"?

- Why do you think it is important to know that our righteousness is *real* because of our new nature, not because God is looking at us "as if" we were righteous?

Talking to Jesus

Jesus, for so long I have looked to other people to tell me who I am. And they look to my accomplishments, the visible. But you say that I have become your righteousness by nature! Remind me, Jesus, of the spiritual surgery that occurred at the center of my being as I was crucified, buried, and then raised with you. Remind me of my spiritual identity, the irrevocable role that I play in your kingdom and in your family. Teach me to see myself with your eyes. Show me who I really am—that I am not my shame—so that I might make choices that truly fulfill me at the core. Amen.

part three

WHEN GUILT AND ANGER RULE

CHAPTER 8

Guilt. Sometimes, a sense of condemnation can be all-consuming. We might think that we deserve to remain in its clutches. Maybe we see it as our penance, our payment for the sins we have committed.

Many of us take to guilt like a devoted servant, as we allow it to command our every move. Perhaps we were overwhelmed with guilt by a parent who shamed us into thinking we should not feel anything different. Or maybe we somehow ended up with a disfigured view of our heavenly Father, and we imagine he wants us to remain under guilt because of our many sins.

Unfortunately, some of our churches aren't much help in this regard. We may continually hear messages or receive subtle signals that guilt is the motivator in the Christian life. We might think that without guilt as a driving force, we simply wouldn't live the lives that God wants us to.

Agreeing with God

Here's a radical thought: the only thing keeping us under that condemning sense of guilt is our choice to ignore the sacrifice of Jesus and instead entertain the accusation of the enemy. So we might allow ourselves to continue *feeling* guilty, but *because of Christ we have been declared innocent*!

The verdict has already been delivered. Because of the work of Jesus Christ, we have been re-created as children of God, free from any law that would condemn us. Instead, we are now under grace and have been declared both holy and blameless (Eph. 1:4; Col. 1:22). "Blameless" means that no one with any real authority is blaming us. So if God himself is not blaming us, calling us guilty, then why should we entertain thoughts of blame and shame about our past?

But some of us have committed a sin that seems so big in our minds that we cannot imagine God could somehow look past it. And he didn't look past it! Instead, he looked right at it before the foundation of the world. He judged us for it. The verdict was guilty. The punishment was death. Yes, death—he took it very seriously. But then Jesus *died* in our place for it. And it is finished!

That's the whole point of the cross.

When we determine that because of the size or quantity of our sins, we are somehow unworthy of God's love, we are spitting in the face of Jesus. We have adopted a standard "higher" than God's. After all, if God is fully satisfied with the sacrifice of his Son, then who are we to disagree with him?

It Is Finished!

Are we really allowed to be motivated purely by our heart's desires in the midst of spiritual freedom? Isn't that condemning sense of guilt deserved, even needed, at least to some degree? These are good questions, but here's a better one.

Are you willing to receive what you don't deserve?

That is what God's healing grace is all about. We have received a forgiveness we could not possibly earn or deserve. So let's embrace grace as God's gift to us. Let's be impressed with the size of that gift, not the size of our sins.

Total, unconditional forgiveness? Yes, the fact is that we are already forgiven for *all* of our sins. God has completely taken away our sins. When we see the finished work of Jesus Christ and its specific effects on our own lives, we realize there is no place left for guilt. Today, on this side of the cross, we are privileged to enjoy a "once for all" forgiveness (Heb. 7:27; 10:10–11) that people under the law could not experience (Heb. 8:6; 11:13). If they had experienced the total, unconditional forgiveness that we enjoy today, then they "would have been *cleansed once for all* and would *no longer have felt guilty* for their sins" (Heb. 10:2).

God's forgiveness of us is a black-and-white issue. It is not that we *might* be forgiven or *could* be forgiven at some future date. No, we *have been* forgiven of *all* our sins—past, present, and future (Col. 2:13; 1 John 2:12).

Some Tough Advice

Nothing can ever separate you from the Healer's tender love for you (Rom. 8:38–39). There is no sin that Jesus did not anticipate and already make full payment for through the cross.

Here's a bit of tough advice for all of us: Since we are forgiven people, how about we decide to get over ourselves and get over the size of our sins? After all, we *are* forgiven people! Let's wake up every day and simply believe in God's great love for us. He most certainly loves us, whether we fully believe it or not. Therefore, why not save ourselves the misery of self-inflicted shame? Why not agree with God about just how effective the sacrifice of his Son really was? The fact is that we are completely forgiven and wholly loved, no matter what!

God has the market cornered on truth. He knows what he is talking about. He has fully evaluated the matter of our sins, and he has determined that we are fully forgiven for all of them. We are wise to adopt his standard, not our own. Our role is to agree with him that the blood of Jesus Christ is enough and that we are forgiven, period. No *ifs* about it.

Are you willing to *choose* to live in the total, unconditional forgiveness that Jesus purchased for you? Amidst the sea of voices out there, the Healer's voice is the only one that really matters. To agree with him about his finished work is to truly honor him.

Questions to Consider

- How many of *your* sins did Jesus die for? So how forgiven are you? To what degree have you agreed with God about the sacrifice of his Son?
- First John 2:2 (NASB) says that Jesus Christ is the "propitiation [satisfying sacrifice] for our sins." What does this mean to you personally?

- We are now holy and blameless before God. What might you still be blaming yourself for? What choice do you need to make that will enable you to stop playing the blame and shame game?
- Reflect on this statement: Confession of sins is healthy and honest, but it does not make you any more forgiven by God. Only blood sacrifice accomplishes forgiveness.

Talking to Jesus

Jesus, I believe that you have taken away all my sins. I see now that God the Father is fully satisfied with your sacrifice. I choose to agree with you that I am a forgiven person, now and forever. It is finished, and I stand before you both holy and blameless because of your finished work, not any work of my own. Remind me, Jesus, to fix my eyes on you and your truth that sets me free. Amen.

CHAPTER 9

We get sick. We grieve the loss of a loved one. We lose our job. Or our spouse abandons us. We instantly try to connect the dots, wondering if maybe God is punishing us for something we did wrong. We self-examine, asking which of our sins caused God to react in such a way.

We buy into a "Christian karma" of sorts.

But the cross shatters the idea of Christian karma. Heaven is not hurling punishment toward us. Our sins have been forgiven—they are forgiven and remembered no more. Because this is true, we need to attribute our illness, our trouble, or our loss to some *other* source, not God. That other source may be the world, the flesh, or the devil. But these difficulties do *not* come from the hand of the One who wants to bring healing in the midst of everything this broken world may throw our way.

Have you been wondering why God would allow a circumstance in your life? Have you permitted the enemy to feed you the lie that maybe God is punishing you in some way? Remember that all of God's punishment for your sins fell on Jesus instead of you. That's a fact. The reason we encounter hard times is simply because we live on planet Earth. God never promised an escape from trouble on *this* side of heaven.

When we project the character of a cruel dictator on our heavenly Father, it becomes difficult for us to see his kind, affectionate smile toward us. We might set up such wrong expectations of him that we cannot imagine him to be any other way. But we need to know the truth about him. We need to taste his goodness toward us. Nothing pleases him more than for us to know how deeply loved (and liked!) we are, and nothing is a greater assurance to us in times of trouble.

Self-Punishment?

Sometimes we might even punish ourselves, thinking that if we are hard on ourselves, maybe God won't be. Much like the young monk Martin Luther once did, we beat up on ourselves (physically or mentally) for what we've done. But once we realize that God is not punishing us now nor at any time in the future, we can cease our attempts to punish ourselves as well. We can stop trying to "make up" for our sins with any sort of self-inflicted condemnation and penitent behavior. We can accept Jesus's payment for our sins and choose to be satisfied just as God is fully satisfied with the finished work of his Son.

This also means we don't have to deny or diminish the damage done. We don't have to engage in excuse making with "It wasn't that bad" or "Nobody really got hurt" or some other justification of our actions. Instead, we can recognize sins for what they are—sins. But at the same time, we can recognize the cross for what it is—the one-time removal of all our sins, meaning we need have no fear of punishment, either now or in the future.

This can also have a big impact on how we treat others. Once we are free from the cycle of "sin, punish, feel better," we can begin to extend the love and grace of God to others around us. We no longer go about judging and seeking to punish people with our withdrawal, silent treatment, or outbursts of anger toward them when they fail. We see that Jesus's death on the cross is the full payment for *their* sins as well, not just our own. Then we can adopt the same attitude toward their failures that God has toward ours. We learn to release them and keep no record of their wrongs.

Forgiven: Now *and* Later!

God remembers our sins no more. Because of our total, unconditional forgiveness, we can have confidence on the day of judgment (1 John 4:17–18). God's Word tells us that Jesus will return one day "without reference to sin" and that we can "eagerly await Him" (Heb. 9:28 NASB).

Why won't Christ even bring up our sins? Because he already took them away "once for all" through the cross (Heb. 10:10). This means that *we will not be judged for any of our sins*. After all, imagine if we were! The wages of sin is death (Rom. 6:23), not just a slap on the hand or less jewelry in heaven. Death. That's why Jesus died—to pay the full wages of sin. So let's do the math and celebrate!

It's true that all humans will appear before the judgment seat of Christ (2 Cor. 5:10), but this is a black-and-white judgment. While unbelievers will be judged for their sins, Christians will be rewarded even for giving a cup of water in Jesus's name (Matt. 10:42). This is *very* different from Christians being judged for our sins. Again, the only verdict would be guilty and the only worthy punishment would be death. That is precisely why Jesus died in our place.

The Healer assures us that "he who believes in Him is not judged" (John 3:18 NASB). So if we have allowed our minds to be filled with thoughts of judgment from God for our sins, we can unabashedly replace those thoughts with new thoughts of confidence. We can eagerly await Jesus's return because "perfect love drives out fear, because *fear has to do with punishment*. The one who fears is not made perfect in love" (1 John 4:18).

This is an important part of the renewing of our minds. Knowing our freedom from any future punishment allows our view of God to be corrected. We discover that he is on our side. We realize that his smiling face is toward us, all the time, both now and forever. God is for us.

Questions to Consider

- Have you ever caught yourself trying to "connect the dots" between your past sins and your difficult circumstances? Did you ever believe this might be God punishing you with "Christian karma" of sorts? How does the finished work of Jesus Christ destroy the idea of "Christian karma"?

- Do you sometimes find yourself denying the reality of your sin struggle? How does understanding our total forgiveness in Christ release us to be more honest and open with God and with trusted friends?
- Have you ever imagined that you might be judged by God for your sins? How does understanding that "the wages of sin is death" (Rom. 6:3) and that Jesus died in your place change all of that for you? What does this powerful truth inspire in you?

Talking to Jesus

Thank you, Jesus, that there is no condemnation for me. You will never refer to my sins again, because you remember them no more. You are not punishing me for them now, nor will you ever! Thank you that the work of the cross destroys any and all sense of "Christian karma" in my life. I am so grateful that I can relax around you, receive your counsel, and no longer live in fear. When earthly circumstances hit, I can know that you are on my side, in my corner, and you are for me. I love you, Jesus, and I thank you for the security of my new covenant relationship with you. Amen.

CHAPTER 10

Betrayal. Abuse. Abandonment. We all get angry with those who hurt us. But sometimes it feels like the anger we feel gets "stuck" at a level 10. It just won't go away, even after a lot of time has passed. What can we do about the buildup of anger, and how does God's soft, healing touch fit into the picture?

Our Empathetic Healer

Anger is an emotion, a feeling. So it's not something we should try to stuff down or stomp out. But *anger typically stems from hurt or fear*. When we find ourselves feeling anger toward someone, it is healthy to stop and ask ourselves how that person might have hurt us or made us fearful. With a bit of reflection, it's usually possible to determine what pain or fear is at the heart of the anger.

So admit you're angry. Don't stuff it down. Express it openly to God. Then ask him to help you recognize the source—the hurt or fear in your life. As we are transparent before the Healer, God's Spirit will reveal to us the *root* of the anger. But once we know the root cause, the action taken by the offender, then what should we *do*?

For starters, know that Jesus can relate to our pain. Yes, our Healer experienced pain like we can never even imagine: Total and undeserved rejection. Physical abuse. Emotional distress. He was an innocent person, murdered for no justifiable reason. Though he had the right to be treated fairly, to be treated like a king, he gave up his rights and experienced unbelievable anguish and pain. Because of this, he is able to empathize with the difficulties we face (Heb. 4:15–16).

Our Healer understands.

It is comforting to know that Jesus can relate to our pain. But how *exactly* do we move forward in a healthy way after being mistreated by others? We might be holding in a great deal of anger and resentment toward those who have offended us. We might believe we have the right to be treated differently, more fairly.

So what is the solution? What is our route to healing?

The Route to Healing

As God's children, we are designed to forgive. Since we now have a new heart, it is actually in our nature to forgive. We are forgiving people, and no other response to our offenders will ever genuinely satisfy us. This is precisely why our Father urges us to forgive others *just as he forgave us* (Eph. 4:32; Col. 3:13).

What do we notice about *how* God forgave us?

1. God *initiated* the forgiveness, not waiting for us to apologize for every sin.
2. God made a *choice* to forgive us and now relates to us in light of that choice.
3. God canceled the debt, *releasing* us from anything we owed him.

This is what real forgiveness looks like. It is a *decision* that we make to *cancel* the debt, *regardless* of whether someone even admits what they did was wrong or owns up to how they hurt us.

This may seem like a hard decision to make, but remember that we are *designed by God to forgive*. We will only be fulfilled at the core when we choose to release others from what they "owe" us. We might think they owe us an apology. We might feel they are indebted to us and should therefore receive retaliation from us as a form of payback. But true forgiveness is a no-strings-attached, total release from *anything* we think they owe us or deserve as "punishment."

Forgiveness Is a Choice

Sometimes we might hesitate to forgive someone because we don't *feel* very forgiving toward them. We might still feel a great deal of anger toward them. So we examine our emotional state and decide we are not in any condition to forgive. We buy into the error that forgiveness is a feeling.

Forgiveness is a choice, *not* a feeling. It is about choosing to cancel a debt owed to us. Yes, we might feel that someone owes us an apology or that they should make up for what they have done to us. They owe us, big-time. *But forgiveness is releasing them from that debt and giving up the right to be treated fairly by them.* Making this choice to forgive may fly in the face of everything we are currently feeling. Our feelings may cry out against the whole idea of forgiveness. Still, we *can* choose. This mirrors what God did when he chose to forgive us.

We don't have to wait for our feelings to come on board. Instead, we can follow the divine sequence that God has given us: *think*, then *choose*, then *feel*. We can set our minds on the truth of what needs to be done. We can choose to forgive and release someone from the debt owed to us. Then, from that day forward, we can remember the choice we made. We can continue to live in agreement with the choice we made. Our emotions may or may not line up with our choice. Still, we *know* what we chose to do—forgive and release—and that is what matters most.

One and Done

Because forgiveness is a choice, it is something that we *do* and then *it's done*. It is not an ongoing, progressive act. Some people hesitate to forgive someone, saying something like, "I'm working on it" or "It may take me a while to completely forgive them." This implies that forgiveness takes time.

It doesn't. While feelings take time to change, forgiveness is only a choice away. Once we decide that we are willing to choose forgiveness, we can complete the act of forgiving immediately.

Have you been waiting to forgive someone until you feel more ready? Are you willing to consider the idea that forgiveness is a choice you can make here and now? In the next chapter, you'll be invited to make the choice to forgive those who have hurt you.

You may be thinking, "But I can't just let them off the hook! They deserve consequences, including my anger at them!" We tend to think that forgiveness is only for the benefit of the *other* person, the offender.

With forgiveness, the benefit to the offender is only half of the truth. Sure, there may be some tangible benefit to someone else when we choose to forgive them, but *forgiveness is many times just for our own benefit*. We forgive so that we don't have to walk around anymore with bitterness or resentment inside. When we forgive, we get to live free of those controlling thoughts. Forgiveness is for our own benefit as much as anyone else's. In fact, the person we forgive may no longer be living or may never even find out that we forgave them! In that case, the benefits of forgiving them are *all* our own.

Questions to Consider

- Do you believe it's possible to forgive someone as a *choice*, even if your feelings disagree with the decision? Why or why not?
- Can you identify any anger you may be holding in? What hurt or fear do you think might be driving that anger?

- How does knowing what Jesus went through—rejection, abuse, distress—help us as we communicate with him about our hurts and fears?
- How does having a new heart as a child of God play into your decision to forgive others?

Talking to Jesus

Jesus, thank you for choosing to forgive me and release me from anything that I owe you. Your forgiveness of me is so all-encompassing, so final. I am so appreciative of the release this brings me. I know that you call me to turn and reflect this kind of forgiveness toward those around me. Help me to remember that I am now a forgiving person by nature. Be my strength as I choose forgiveness of those who have hurt me. Thank you for the genuine freedom and enduring peace that my choice to forgive can bring. Amen.

CHAPTER 11

How *exactly* do we forgive? Do we somehow push the Delete button in our minds, magically erasing the anger and pain we feel? Do we pretend our feelings don't even exist or don't matter? If any of these were true, there would be no way that any of us could truly forgive!

Assessing the emotional damage is important. What events occurred? How did those events make you feel? Then, once we have assessed the damage, we simply make the *choice* to forgive the offender, releasing them from anything they owe us. Finally, we might thank God for the privilege of forgiving them and ask him to remind us of the decision we made. So once you've found a quiet place where you can be alone with God, here's what to do.

1. **Assess the damage:** *It hurt me when he/she. . . . It made me feel (embarrassed, abandoned, rejected, etc.) . . .*
2. **Choose to forgive and release the debt:** *But I choose, as an act of my will, because I am a forgiving person in Christ, to forgive him/her and release him/her from anything that he/she owes me, even if he/she does it again.*
3. **Remember your choice:** *Thank you, Lord Jesus Christ, for the opportunity to forgive (name of offender). I ask you to remind me, in the moments I need it the most, of this decision I made today.*

   (Note: Some people prefer to place an empty chair in front of them and imagine the offender sitting in it. Then they speak *directly* to the offender in the empty chair, saying, "It hurt me when *you*. . . . I choose to forgive *you* and release *you*. . . . even if *you* do it again." This empty chair method is simply a different way of carrying out the same forgiveness process.)

Did you notice that the forgiveness statement says "even if he/she does it again"? Of course, this does *not* mean that we want it to happen again. Neither does it mean that what the person did to us was okay. It simply means that we are *fully* forgiving them with an *unconditional* release from anything they owe us, with no strings attached. This is the only real way to move forward and experience healing from past hurts inflicted by those around us.

Who Can Be on Our List?

When it comes to family members, it is often hard to even admit they have hurt us. It might feel like we are betraying them in some way. "It's my job to stay strong for the sake of the family," we might think. But remember that it is *not* our job to "be strong" with God. Our role is to be transparent and human before the Healer, telling him about our pain and allowing him to lead us through the process of forgiveness *in a healthy way*.

We might live in denial of the hurt we are feeling from someone. At times, this denial can even have a "spiritual" look to it with a statement like, "Well, I love them and want the best for them, despite what they did. I'm already praying for them!" But praying for someone is *not* the same as assessing the damage they have done to us and releasing them from anything they owe us, even if they do it again. We should put anyone who has brought pain into our lives on the list of people we need to forgive.

Next, we shouldn't hesitate to put *God* on our list of those to forgive. God? Yes, God. While God is never guilty of doing anything wrong, forgiveness is *not always* about forgiving someone who has purposely or actually wronged us. Sometimes people hurt or disappoint us when they *fall short of our own unrealistic expectations for them*.

Maybe you need to forgive God for allowing something painful to happen in your life when you expected him to step in and prevent it. Good examples might be the loss of a loved one, the loss of a job, an illness, or an injury. While we can chalk these up to the fallen world we live in, it is often hard for us to understand why God allows these things to go on. We do sometimes hold unrealistic expectations of God, so we can forgive him for not meeting those expectations. In other words, we release him from anything that we *thought* he owed us. We do this for our own benefit, not God's. We do this to be free of anything we have wrongly held against God.

Lastly, we might need to put *ourselves* on the list of people to forgive. Sometimes we embarrass ourselves, bring harm on ourselves, and fall short of our own expectations. Then we find it difficult to live with ourselves, given what we have done. We need to forgive and release ourselves from anything that we think we owe ourselves. When we let ourselves off the hook, we extend the same grace to ourselves that God extended to us. We align our thinking with his.

Forgiveness ≠ Forgetting

Forgiveness is *not* forgetting. We cannot literally erase the memories in our brain. We may always have a memory of events that hurt us, but forgiveness does not mean forgetting.

God, who says he will remember our sins no more (Heb. 8:12; 10:17), is not some forgetful old man who accidentally misplaced them. No, God simply chooses not to hold our sins against us in any way. So forgiveness means we choose not to hold an offense against someone, not that we actually forget it happened. Even when we truly forgive them, we may still have a memory of the event for a long time. That is normal, to be expected, and no indicator of whether we truly forgave them.

Regardless of what we feel or what memories may pass through our mind, we can always remember the *choice* we made to forgive. We can recall the day we put the stake in the ground and declared the offender to be free from anything they owe us. This is how we mirror God's forgiveness of us. This is the only route to freedom from anger and bitterness. This is the only path to healing from our hurts.

Questions to Consider

- Why do you think it might be important to properly assess the damage before choosing to forgive?
- Has God ever disappointed you by not meeting your expectations? Will you consider putting God on your list of those to forgive?
- Sometimes it is hardest to forgive ourselves. Make sure to put yourself on the list of people to forgive. What things might you need to forgive yourself for?
- How does it help us to know that forgiveness does not mean forgetting?
- Consider taking some time alone with God to go through the steps of forgiveness outlined in this chapter. Give yourself enough time to make a thorough list of offenders and ways you've been hurt.

Talking to Jesus

Jesus, I ask you to bring to mind those people in my life whom I need to forgive in order to truly walk free from the anger and resentment that have impacted my life. Reveal to me the hurt and fear that are beneath my anger. Guide me through this important decision to forgive and release people from anything they owe me, even if they do it again. Jesus, show me how I can also forgive myself for self-inflicted damage I have caused in my life. Thank you for being my strength as I choose to forgive. Amen.

part four

WHEN TEMPTATION WINS

CHAPTER 12

Accusation. God's Word says you have an enemy who accuses you "day and night" (Rev. 12:10). Accusation requires ammunition. Your track record is the enemy's ammunition. Right after a failure on your part, the enemy heaps on the guilt, the mental images, the condemnation, the name-calling, and the shame.

He wants you to wallow in your failure. So how do you respond?

You are not defined by one sin here or there. You are not defined by a multitude of sins. You are not your performance. And now that you are in Christ, you are not sinful.

Yes, we all commit sins, but we as children of God are not sinful by nature. God did not re-create us in Christ Jesus as dirty, rotten sinners. He re-created us as cleansed, *righteous* saints (2 Cor. 5:21; Eph. 2:10) who are now holy and blameless (Eph. 1:4; Col. 1:22).

(Note: If you're wondering how you can have daily sin struggles but still be righteous by nature, we will address that soon!)

Forgiving Ourselves in the Moment

Right after a sin failure, do you forgive yourself just as God forgave you? Or do you tune in to accusation and adopt the enemy's view of you? Our response to accusation after committing a sin reveals what we believe about ourselves and about God's view of us.

We might buy the lie that sin causes a rift between us and God. But if we are God's children, holy and blameless before him, then his voice is unwavering as he reminds us that, when it comes to our sins, he will "remember no more" (Heb. 10:17). God is simply not dealing with us on the basis of our sins—at all.

Yes, there is a healthy regret of sin, as we are not designed for it! And God cares about our behavior. But any guilt and shame that we take on flies in the face of all that Jesus accomplished on the cross. There is now no condemnation of any kind for us (Rom. 8:1). So here's our challenge for you:

Stop beating yourself up for your failures.

God isn't beating you up, so why are you? Do you have the right to be harder on yourself than God is? Instead, focus your attention on the blood of Jesus Christ and realize you are *still* clean and close to God. You may have acted in a way that is contrary to your true identity, but you are still clean and close to him, *no matter what*. Release any and all guilt, completely, in light of the blood of Jesus Christ. "You are a totally forgiven person"—these are the Healer's words to you in the midst of accusation.

Saying No to Temptation

But what about the next time we confront temptation? How can we learn to respond differently? Real change begins with *properly understanding the source of temptation.*

God is essentially inviting us to reinterpret our entire thought lives. Just because we have a thought swirling around in our heads does not mean that the thought originated with us. God has shown us in his Word that there are other sources of the thoughts we might receive. One of these sources is called "the flesh."

What exactly is the flesh?

When you buy a new computer, you take it home, pull it out of the box, and plug it in. Next thing you know, you're online and working away. But within minutes, your computer starts asking you if you'd like to update your software.

"But I just got this computer. It's brand-new!" you might think.

Yeah, you've got shiny new hardware all right, but the software that runs on it is not always new. So you're confronted with the option of downloading an update or clicking that little X to close the window and decline it.

At salvation, we get brand-new spiritual hardware—a new heart, a new spirit, and God's Spirit living in us. But we still experience the daily renewing of our minds. That's like those software updates. We have a choice: we can choose to *accept* or *decline* those updates. This is why the Healer counsels us to "not conform to the pattern of this world, but be transformed by the renewing of your mind" (Rom. 12:2).

Those old, unrenewed mindsets are what the Bible calls "the flesh." Those are the ways in which we might *naturally* cope in this world apart from the Healer's counsel. That old programming pulls at us to do things the old way, rather than getting the updated thinking we really desire from God's Spirit (Gal. 5:17).

Remember that the flesh is *not* our spiritual hardware. The flesh is *not* our spiritual nature. The flesh is *not* the core of our being. No, at the core we are children of God, born of the Spirit, with new spiritual hardware! So the flesh is like that old software. It's old thinking that needs to be replaced, but it's not you. If you take just one lesson from this chapter, we hope it is this: *you are not the flesh*.

While we all struggle with the flesh, we are not defined by it. It is the old way to *think* and *act* (Rom. 8:5–6), but it is *not* us. We are new creations. We are not the source of struggle with sin. This is why God tells us to walk not according to the flesh but instead according to his Spirit (Gal. 5:16). He is calling us to be ourselves (be who we really are!) and not be deluded into identifying ourselves with the flesh.

Our role in the battle is to hear God's Spirit bearing witness to our true identity as "the Spirit himself testifies with our spirit that we are God's children" (Rom. 8:16). In this way, we can wake up every day, keep in step with his Spirit, and simply be ourselves. This *informed* decision making is how we begin to walk in the truth of who we *really* are and find victory over nagging temptation.

Questions to Consider

- How do you typically feel after you've sinned? Do you often allow your mind to transition from a *godly regret* to a *condemning guilt*?

- In what ways is God inviting us to a radical paradigm shift in how we look at our entire thought life?
- In your own words, can you give a definition of the flesh?
- If someone were to ask you how you can be a righteous new creation, born of God's Spirit, but still be tempted by sinful thoughts, could you give a good answer? (Hint: Think about your new spiritual "hardware" versus the "software updates.")

Talking to Jesus

Jesus, I feel the pull of the flesh every day. It scares me when the tempting thoughts pass through my mind. But I thank you that I am not the flesh. Thank you for giving me a brand-new life in your Spirit. I ask for you to coach me in my true identity so that I can begin reinterpreting my entire thought life. Show me that I am not the sum total of the thoughts that pass through my mind. Reveal to me that I am clean and close to you, seated now at your right hand. Teach me how to set my mind on the truth of who I really am and to enjoy walking in step with you. Amen.

CHAPTER 13

Porn, drug abuse, fantasy, envy, an affair—secret sins that maybe no one knows about. Sin gets a foothold in our lives, and we panic. It goes on for some time, and we wonder if we will ever be free. We feel like we have tried everything—accountability partners, prayer, Bible reading, maybe even spiritual warfare deliverance!

Our Christian friends might tell us, "Just repent. Stop doing it out of your love for God." That only makes us feel worse! For some reason, we can't seem to stop. Is something wrong with us? Are we just different? Did God somehow forget to equip us with his power while everyone else got the proper dosage?

We Need a Game Plan

Within hours of the 9/11 terrorist attacks, President George W. Bush delivered a televised speech to the

American people. In his speech, he detailed the events that had occurred and put forth a message of hope—a game plan to seek out those who had perpetrated the crimes and bring them down. On that day, our military began the long process of tracking down the terrorists and bringing their organizations to an end.

But what if the president had articulated no plan at all? Imagine if he had simply said, "Some tragic events have occurred, and I don't have a clue how to proceed. We are open to any suggestions you might have out there." That certainly would have sent the whole country into fear and despair!

It's no different in our struggle with sin. We need a game plan. We need to know who the enemy is and how to approach the battle.

The Game Plan

There is no magic wand or secret formula that leads to automatic victory over sin struggles in our lives. But there is *an informed choice* we can make. Along with that choice, there is *the power of God's Spirit* in our lives. But what is the informed choice, and how exactly is God's Spirit leading us in the moment of temptation? What is the truth that sets us free from nagging temptations that slam us every day?

There is a spiritual battle taking place, and our minds are the battlefield. But who are the opponents? The Bible tells us that "*the flesh* sets its desire against *the Spirit*, and the Spirit against the flesh; for these are in opposition to one another, so that *you* may not do the things that you please" (Gal. 5:17 NASB). Notice the two opponents: the flesh and the Spirit. So where are you in this equation? Apparently, you are a bystander who sometimes ends up not doing the things that you really want to do!

Here's a newsflash: *it's not our job to fight the flesh.* Notice that Galatians 5 tells us that God's Spirit is the one who battles against the flesh on our behalf. Maybe you've tried to fight the flesh. Maybe you've wondered why you can't seem to overcome it. You've tried to employ Approach 1:

Approach 1: Me in the middle

flesh →← me ← God's Spirit

But the Bible never tells us to be strong. It tells us to "be strong *in the Lord* and in the strength of *His* might" (Eph. 6:10 NASB). Apparently, the battle belongs to him. Wait a minute, though—we do play a role in this somehow, don't we? Yes, God's Word says this is our role: "*walk by the Spirit*, and you will not carry out the desire of the flesh" (Gal. 5:16 NASB). *Our role is to walk by the Spirit*. He fights the fight, and we simply keep in step with him.

Approach 2: Me walking by God's Spirit

flesh →← God's Spirit

me

Don't get caught in the middle, trying to fight a battle that belongs to the Spirit. Instead, walk *alongside* him. Keep in step with him, listening to his counsel and letting him be your focus along the way.

Two Ways to Walk

We humans are never in control. We were designed by God to always be controlled (inspired) by an outside force. At any given moment, we are either *walking by the flesh* or we are *walking by God's Spirit*. There is no third way to walk.

The beauty of this is that *everything is spiritual*. We might normally think of our activities as belonging to one of three categories:

- Category 1: spiritual acts (attending church, studying the Bible, sharing your faith, etc.)
- Category 2: sinful acts (jealous acts, sexual sins, outbursts of anger, etc.)

- Category 3: neutral acts (brushing your teeth, shopping, etc.)

But this is *not* the way God's Word describes the human experience for Christians. We as children of God have *only two* ways to walk, not three:

Walk 1: by the Spirit
Walk 2: by the flesh

There is no third way to walk. This means that everything we do *can* be an expression of Christ within us. Also, everything we do can be an expression of the flesh. Therefore, everything is "spiritual" in some way, because we are spiritual at the core. There are no neutral acts. Whether you're brushing your teeth or shopping or playing video games, all of these can be done according to the Spirit or according to the flesh. This also means that many church-related activities can be done with a healthy "want-to" motivation (walking by the Spirit) or with an unhealthy "have-to" or "look at me" motivation (walking by the flesh).

The bottom line in seeing this truth is that our real goal is *not* to increase the quantity of church activity or to decrease the quantity of neutral acts. No, the goal is to know Jesus Christ in *everything* we do. We are to realize that he wants to be *life* to us in all our activities, whether church-related or not.

Remember that long before there were Bibles or churches, there were two people in the Garden of Eden. They lost life. In Jesus Christ, we receive back what they lost. God's greatest desire is for us to *know him* and to believe that he has given us *everything* we need for every aspect of life through relationship with his Son, Jesus Christ (Phil. 3:10; 2 Pet. 1:3).

Choosing is not easy. The old ways of the flesh are much like an elaborate set of highways that has been built up over time. Those highways may be six lanes wide! Imagine choosing to exit from a well-traveled, six-lane highway and then driving down what feels like a little rabbit trail just being formed. Sure, over time that little rabbit trail will start to widen and feel more familiar, but it *does* take time. And it does require the tough choice to travel a new path. But our new identity means that, one way or another, that new path is our destiny!

Questions to Consider

- Is there some sin that you feel has a hold in your life? How important do you think it is to have a game plan concerning your struggle?

- Have you tried to "fight the flesh" at times? In what ways? What was the outcome of the fight?
- What does it mean to you to walk by the Spirit? How is this different from you trying to fight off the desires of the flesh?
- Had you ever thought about the two ways to walk before? How does understanding that there is no third walk (no "neutral" category) change the way you look at your everyday life?

Talking to Jesus

Jesus, I can see it now. I have been trying to fight the flesh and win the battle. But it's not my fight. The battle belongs to your Spirit. Remind me, Jesus, that there are only two ways to walk and that in every moment I can keep in step with you. Thank you for your presence and your power within me. Thank you for all that you do for me, in me, and through me. I gratefully submit to you and allow you to take the lead in my life. You always lead me to freedom, Jesus, and I cannot thank you enough. Amen.

CHAPTER 14

In 2007, a woman in Phoenix, Arizona, was experiencing equilibrium problems, difficulty in swallowing, and a tingling sensation in her left arm. Doctors performed an MRI on her brain and thought they found a tumor. But once they began the operation to remove the tumor, they actually found it to be a parasite living in her brain! Once doctors successfully removed the parasite, all of her symptoms went away. According to recent medical research, parasites in the brain are more common than we might think.

According to God's Word, a power called "sin" (Greek: *hamartia*) operates within us much like a parasite. This power of sin is very different from *sins*, plural, which are acts of sin. It's even different from the verb *to sin*. What we are talking about here is an intelligent, personified power or principle that is the source of temptation. We are talking about *sin as an active tempter*.

If you've been wondering how you could be such a sincere, eager child of God and yet still have sinful thoughts run through your mind, then understanding the presence of this power called sin can certainly help clear things up. Notice exactly how the apostle Paul describes the conflict within him: "It is *no longer I myself who do it, but it is sin* living in me. . . . Now if I do what I do not want to do, it is *no longer I who do it, but it is sin* living in me that does it" (Rom. 7:17, 20).

Paul announces the same thing twice here: "it is no longer I . . . but it is sin living in me." Paul discovered a power that was acting through the members of his body (v. 23), causing him to do what he didn't really want to do. Paul discovered a tempter parasite called sin. How often do you pause to consider that not every thought that floats through your mind is coming from you?

The Barking Dog

There was once a little girl who didn't want to play in her own backyard. It wasn't that she didn't enjoy the yard. She certainly did! But the next-door neighbors had recently purchased a dog—a big dog with a very loud bark.

The girl's parents called the neighbors repeatedly to ask if the dog might only be let out at certain hours of the day, so the girl could play in peace. But the neighbors wouldn't agree to any such plan, and so the dog stood in that yard barking at the girl through the fence any time she'd go outside of her house.

After this went on for a while, the girl's father devised a plan. He built a six-foot fence between his yard and his neighbor's yard. Then he took his young daughter out into the yard and walked toward the neighbor's house. The dog began barking, of course, and the girl pulled on her daddy's hand to go back in the house. But her daddy urged her to go all the way up to the fence and examine the situation more closely.

Once the girl got to the fence, she realized that the dog was now all bark and no bite. She could play in the yard whenever she wanted, free of concern. Sure, the dog would do what dogs do—bark. But the only real power the dog held over the girl was the power she *gave* to the dog any time she chose to fear its bark.

Dead to Sin, Alive to God

Because of our new identity in Christ, the power of sin is now all bark and no bite. At salvation, we Christians were sealed with the Holy Spirit (Eph. 4:30)—that's the fence. Just like the girl who stood safely in her yard, protected by the fence, we have no cause for alarm now. We are safe from the enemy. He cannot touch us: "the One who was born of God keeps them safe, and the evil one cannot harm them" (1 John 5:18).

The truth is that the power of sin can only make us *think* it can do harm to us. It is important to realize just how impotent the power of sin really is and how powerful our God is: "the one who is in you is greater than the one who is in the world" (1 John 4:4).

No, the power of sin is not dead. It is still very much alive in the world today, and it can "bark" at us at any time. But we are dead *to* sin. We don't have to fear its bite anymore. In other words, *it's on the other side of the spiritual fence*. Sure, we might quiver in fear and run around our yard acting like a victim, thinking, "Who let the dog out?" But no matter how we might feel in a given moment, the truth is still the truth: sin *is* behind the fence, and it's all bark and no bite.

The Fence

Father/Son/Holy Spirit	the flesh
me	the power of sin

While we sometimes find ourselves reacting to sin in the choices we make, the reality is that *we don't have to*. We are now dead to its power and alive to the power of God: "In the same way, count yourselves dead to sin but alive to God in Christ Jesus" (Rom. 6:11).

Why This Matters

Why is it so important to understand the presence of sin and our death to it? If we are going to have a proper self-image, in agreement with what the Healer says about us, then we need to be able to explain where those sinful thoughts really come from!

Many of us Christians have found ourselves taking on an identity that is actually the identity of sin! We might call ourselves depressed people, alcoholics, or sex addicts. We define ourselves by this "disorder" or that one. These are identities we take on as our own, but what we may not realize is that the source of our struggle is not our own spiritual nature. The desires we give in to belong to something else entirely: "Therefore do not let *sin* reign in your mortal body so that you obey *its* evil desires" (Rom. 6:12).

Notice to whom the evil desires belong: the tempter called sin. The Healer is not calling us to say no to ourselves. He is calling us to say no to sin and to say yes to who we truly are!

Did God crucify you, bury you, and raise you as a new creation in Christ but forget to regenerate the "gossip" or "lustful" part of you? Of course not! The reason we still struggle with these things is because *sin did not die*, but instead we died *to* sin. Now we are dead to sin and alive to God, and we're getting our minds renewed to this powerful reality. We really are free from sin's power, not needing to give in to any of the loud barks directed at us.

Do you realize which side of the fence you're on?

Questions to Consider

- How does understanding the presence of a sin "parasite" as the source of temptation help you understand your true identity better?
- Is the idea of "no longer I, but sin" just a chance for excuse making—"the devil made me do it"? Read Romans 6:12. How are we still responsible for what happens in our lives?
- What does it mean to you that the power of sin is "all bark and no bite"?
- How does recognizing which side of the fence you are on affect how you look at yourself and your closeness to God in the midst of temptation or even failure?

Talking to Jesus

Jesus, I realize now that we are on the same team, always. You are never against me. It is you and me in a beautiful union as you have come to live with me and in me, no matter what. The power of sin would have me believe that I am no different from anyone else and that I want to sin. But every time I submit to sin, I only find misery. I want your ways, Jesus. I want your life expressed in me. You have the market cornered on true fulfillment, and I am only satisfied by you. Thank you that no matter what I might feel in times of temptation, I am now dead to sin and alive to you forever. Amen.

part five

WHEN LIFE IS JUST TOO HARD

CHAPTER 15

When we find that perfect someone, we might think they will be the answer to all our problems. They make us feel so good about ourselves. They fill us up. But within months or years, we find out they do not make us whole. We discover that *everyone* around us is made of glass, and that glass does come shattering down at some point.

We expect our best friend to always be there for us, always listen, always sympathize, always put our interests first. But as time passes, we realize they have a life of their own, a set of needs they too are looking to get met. They are not the answer.

A wife looks to her husband to be home from work on time, to spend enough time with her, to romance her, to make her feel important, to do the "little things" that spell love for her. A husband looks to his wife to be his biggest supporter, to respect him, to praise him for his accomplishments, and to be dynamite in bed.

Both the husband and the wife fall short of these expectations. They fail because they are only human. They fail because they themselves are needy and wanting. They fail because they are the creation, not the Creator. Imagine expecting a human to fill the role of God! That is what we are doing when we look to others to meet our needs.

You might have heard that marriage is about two people coming together to complete one another. Quoting the movie *Jerry Maguire*, men might joke to their wives, "You complete me!" or might say of their wives, "She is my better half." But can our spouse truly "complete" us? Are they our "better half"? These expressions imply that we cannot be whole apart from another human being.

The reality is that we are not two halves that complete each other, making a whole. If we set up this expectation in our minds, we will be sorely disappointed with the other person when they fail to "complete" us in a satisfying way.

The only way our interpersonal relationships can really work is when each person is getting their wholeness, their fullness, from Jesus Christ. Otherwise, we simply suck the life out of the other person, as much as we can, until they burn out and have nothing left to give.

The Paradigm Shift

We set up unrealistic expectations for other people to meet our needs. And when they fail, we grow disillusioned, if not angry or depressed. We say things like, "He no longer makes me happy" or "The magic is gone." We arrive at these conclusions because we were looking to the person for more than they could ever give.

So what if the core of the problem is not them? What if the real problem is where we are looking? What if our approach was doomed to fail from the outset? And what if our real needs are *spiritual* in nature?

Sure, it's healthy to be open and honest about our needs. The needs that we feel within us may be very real needs that were given to us by God. But maybe our problem is the way we have gone about getting those needs met. When we look to the creation, rather than the Creator, we will surely be disappointed. The performance of those around us will simply never satisfy.

What we need is a dramatic paradigm shift to start getting our needs met from Christ, who lives within us: "And my God will meet all your needs according to the riches of his glory in Christ Jesus" (Phil. 4:19). Notice *where* these needs are met. They are not met in another human, not in a friend or a spouse or any other created being. They are met *in* Christ Jesus.

This is the plain truth concerning how you'll know true fulfillment in this life. And this is the *only* way to bring real hope to a human relationship that seems to be spiraling downward. As you look to Christ alone, this frees you in the relationship to be yourself and to fully accept the other person, whether or not they have "performed" well in the relationship lately. It means your friendships, your dating relationships, and your marriage (or singlehood) becomes about reaching out and loving others rather than trying to get something from them to fill you up. It means you can participate in relationships as someone who is already full and not left needing more, because "in Him you have been made *complete*" (Col. 2:10 NASB).

Is this radical way to think even possible to live out? We believe it's not only possible, but it can become *normal* for us as children of God. After all, who ever told us to look to those around us to get our needs met? From the very beginning we were intended to draw life from God and from him alone. When we forget this simple truth, often it is one single day in this broken world that can serve as a powerful reminder of where to fix our eyes once again.

Filled by God Himself

Relationships as God designed them are to take place between two complete and whole people who are unable to meet each other's needs. We simply don't have the resources within ourselves to crank out enough "life" to fill another person. Instead, both people need to angle the mirror of their soul elsewhere, toward Christ, to reflect and experience wholeness as he intends. This is a healthy relationship as God intended it from the beginning. This is a Christ-focused relationship inspired by his Spirit living within us.

This is not a life that is mystical or far off. It is normal life as the Creator designed it. We are born empty. At salvation, Christ fills us. It simply makes no sense to look outside of ourselves, to another person, to get further filled. Instead, the Bible tells us to "be filled" continually by God's Spirit (Eph. 5:18). He is our Source and the only One who fills us to the "whole measure of the fullness of Christ" (Eph. 4:13).

Questions to Consider

- In what ways have you looked to the creation (someone else) rather than to the Creator to get your needs met? How have others fallen short?

- Would you be willing to consider the idea that your core needs in life are actually *spiritual* in nature and can only be met by God?
- In this chapter, you learned that looking to the Creator to get your needs met involves a "dramatic paradigm shift." What specifically might this shift look like in your life?
- Have you ever been in a dating relationship or in a marriage where you expected your partner to "complete" you? How might understanding our completeness in Christ help any relationship be healthier?

Talking to Jesus

Jesus, so many people have disappointed me. They fall short of my expectations, and I end up frustrated, disappointed, even depressed. You are the only true constant in my life. Thank you for your never-ending presence with me and in me. Remind me to look to you, the Creator, and not to the creation, to get my needs met. I believe you have equipped me with everything I need for life. I believe you have made me full and complete. I believe you are enough for me. I love you, Jesus. Amen.

CHAPTER 16

A recent survey of Americans revealed that about one-third of us admit to feeling lonely in life. And the statistics for married people aren't much different! Apparently, a lot of us are lonely, and simply finding someone to marry doesn't help much. The only real cure for our loneliness is the constant presence of Someone with us.

This is precisely what God provides through his Holy Spirit—his *constant* presence.

We all spell love in different ways, as there are many "love languages" out there. One of those love languages is time spent. People know that you care about them when you choose to spend time with them.

God has decided to live within each one of us through the person of Jesus Christ. He has decided to spend every moment of our lives with us, as we have been filled with his Spirit within our own human spirit. This is time spent with us. God is communicating his deep love for us by choosing to stick with us no matter how many sins we might commit and no matter what we might experience in this world. He *never* leaves us. He *never* forsakes us (Heb. 13:5).

So eternal life is not just some ticket to heaven. And eternal life is not our life added onto, our life made longer. No, having eternal life means receiving an altogether *different* life—Christ's life.

God didn't just clean house, he moved in! God's presence is now *within* us. We aren't firing up long distance phone calls to a God far away in heaven. God is now up close and personal. And the calls are *local*.

Once we realize that God has secured the presence of his Spirit within us, forever and without conditions, we can begin to fathom just how much he really loves us. We begin to grow convinced that we are lovable, and our deepest emotional wounds can then be healed by his love. We are never alone, and the one who remains with us always is our Healer.

What to *Do*

God's healing message of grace is so much more than God being *with* us. God is not just with us—Christ is *in* us. His presence and his life-changing power reside within us, here and now.

But where does that leave us? What is *our* role? Interestingly, God's Word often uses the word "let" in describing our role in the relationship.

- *Let* your light shine before others. (Matt. 5:16)
- *Let* this mind be in you, which was also in Christ Jesus. (Phil. 2:5 KJV)
- *Let* your gentle spirit be known to all men. (Phil. 4:5 NASB)
- *Let* the peace of Christ rule in your hearts. (Col. 3:15 NASB)
- *Let* the word of Christ richly dwell within you. (Col. 3:16 NASB)

We are always looking for something to *do, do, do*. We might be so preoccupied with working for God that we fail to see that *he is working in us*. Through the new covenant—our total forgiveness, our freedom from the law, and our union with Christ—God has rigged everything. He has set up everything in advance so that he can live in us, 24-7, without interruption. Our only real job is to *let* him shine through us!

Beyond What We Can Bear?

You may have heard the idea that God will not allow you to experience anything beyond what you can bear. But haven't we all come up against circumstances that were just too much for us? The result was significant pain and heartache.

The reality is that God never promised that this world would be smooth sailing. While he does say that we won't be tempted (with sin) unless there is a way to escape that sinful choice (1 Cor. 10:13), plenty of Christians, today and historically, have experienced hardships they felt *very* unready for!

Notice the way Paul describes his troubles: "We do not want you to be uninformed, brothers and sisters, about the troubles we experienced in the province of Asia. We were under great pressure, *far beyond our ability to endure*, so that we despaired of life itself. . . . This happened *that we might not rely on ourselves but on God*" (2 Cor. 1:8–9).

Why would God allow things to come into our lives that we simply cannot bear? Well, here's a better question to consider: How in the world would we ever learn a deeper dependency on him *without* experiencing troubles too great for us to handle?

If we carry an unrealistic expectation that we will have a life of smooth sailing or even tolerable circumstances, then when life hits us hard, we will be confused, if not totally disillusioned. This is why it's important to understand that we were never promised an easy life just because we believe in Jesus. In fact, Jesus himself told us, "In this world you will have trouble" (John 16:33). And Peter tells us not to be surprised by a fiery ordeal that comes upon us (1 Pet. 4:12).

Once our thinking aligns with the truth that we *will* indeed encounter circumstances that we cannot bear, we'll no longer be confused by our unrealistic expectations not being met. Instead, we can then relinquish our so-called rights to cushy circumstances and easy living and instead find real peace within the Healer himself. *Real peace is experienced not with the arrival of new circumstances but with the arrival of new covenant thinking, even when old circumstances remain.*

He Will Do It *All*!

We encounter difficult times "that we might not rely on ourselves but on God" (2 Cor. 1:9). So next time you encounter a circumstance that you cannot seem to handle, what if, rather than trying to handle it, you actually admitted that you can't handle it? And what if, instead of resorting to escapism, you asked God to be your strength, your comfort, and your inspiration in the midst of it all?

The Healer is ready. His power is made perfect in our weakness (2 Cor. 12:9). We can lay down our weaknesses before him, and he can be our strength. Does this mean that all of our troubles go away? No, it simply means that we may be "hard pressed on every side, but not crushed" (2 Cor. 4:8).

It is *not* our strength plus God's strength. He is not wanting us to try to get stronger. Instead, he wants us to abandon our independent sense of strength, exchanging it for all that he is, in and through us. He will do it all *for* you. He will do it all *in* you. He will do it all *through* you.

Questions to Consider

- Do you honestly believe that God the Healer can be the solution to your loneliness? To what degree?
- In this chapter, you learned that eternal life is not your former life made longer. Instead, eternal life is actually Christ's life. So in practical terms, what does it mean to you to have eternal life?
- Had you ever thought about the difference between firing up "long distance phone calls" to heaven versus Christ being in you? What difference might this make in your daily life? In your prayer life?

- How does the "let" concept differ from some more common views of how to make the Christian life work?
- Contrary to popular belief, God's Word tells us that we may sometimes experience more than we can bear in life. Has that ever happened to you? What did you learn through the circumstance?

Talking to Jesus

Jesus, you are so willing to lead me, guide me, counsel me, and help me. You have set up everything so that your presence is always guaranteed in my life. Thank you for being the cure to my loneliness. Sometimes life seems so unbearable, so hard. Now I realize that it is indeed unbearable for me, and that I was never meant to bear it. Thank you for not asking me to get stronger, more capable. Thank you for being my strength in every storm. Remind me to look to you as my source. Teach me what it means that you are my Life, now and forever. Amen.

EPILOGUE

God spells *healing* c-o-v-e-n-a-n-t.

God's new covenant message of *forgiveness*, *freedom*, and *identity* is the *only* way for us to experience genuine healing. Without a solid understanding of the new covenant, we are left with whatever thoughts and subsequent feelings might float our way. Our thinking needs a reliable source, a rock-solid foundation. The truths of God's new covenant *are* that foundation. Jesus himself *is* that foundation. It is only when the Son sets us free that we are really free (John 8:36).

Are we totally forgiven or only partially forgiven for our sins? Are we completely under grace, or should we balance grace with a law mentality? Are we really new creations with new, clean hearts, or are we half new, half old? These are questions that deserve clear, biblical answers. It's only through God's new covenant message that we find those answers.

We are forgiven, no matter what. We're now designed for God's system of grace, not law. And we are new creations, each of us with a new heart, a new spirit, and God's Spirit living within us. With these powerful truths as our "filter" for every thought we might entertain, God's goodness shines so much brighter.

It is our prayer that God has used this book to reveal how he can be the Healer of your many hurts. If there is someone dear to your heart who you think might benefit from what is written here, consider passing it along. It would mean the world to us to have the privilege of sharing God's healing grace with them.

No matter what trouble you might be facing right now, our desire is that you know that you're always in good company. *The Father* has blessed you with every spiritual blessing (Eph. 1:3). *The Son* is not ashamed to call you brother or sister (Heb. 2:11). And *the Spirit* testifies that you are born of him (Rom. 8:16). The entire Trinity is pleased to have you. You are deeply loved, you are completely forgiven, and you are never, ever alone.

THE HURT & THE HEALER SCRIPTURE GUIDE

My Life under Grace

- I'm dead to the law. (Rom. 7:4, 6; Gal. 2:19)
- I'm not under the law. (Rom. 6:14; Gal. 5:18)
- I'm not supervised by the law. (Gal. 3:25)
- The law's requirements have been fully met in me. (Rom. 8:3–4)
- Christ is the end of the law for me. (Rom. 10:4)
- God's grace is enough to motivate me. (2 Cor. 12:9; Titus 2:11–12)

My New Identity in Christ

- My old self is dead, buried, and gone. (Rom. 6:6–7; Gal. 2:20)
- I'm dead to sin and alive to God. (Rom. 6:11)
- I'm a new creation, born of God's Spirit. (2 Cor. 5:17; 1 John 5:4, 18)
- The source of temptation is sin, not me. (Rom. 6:12; 7:17, 20)
- I'm more than a conqueror through Jesus Christ. (Rom. 8:37)

My "Once for All" Forgiveness

- God forgave me and canceled my debt to him. (Col. 2:13–14)
- I've been forgiven once for all. (Heb. 9:28; 10:2)
- By one sacrifice I've been perfectly cleansed forever. (Heb. 10:14)
- I've been made holy through Jesus's sacrifice. (Heb. 10:10)
- I've been fully reconciled to God. (Eph. 2:16; Col. 1:22)

My Closeness to Christ

- Having eternal life is having Christ's life. (John 17:3; 1 John 5:12)
- Christ literally and actually lives in me. (2 Cor. 13:5; Gal. 2:20)
- Christ and I are spiritually united. (Rom. 6:5; 1 Cor. 6:17)
- God is at work in me, carrying me to completion. (Phil. 1:6; 2:13)
- I serve in God's new way, led by his Spirit. (Rom. 7:6; Gal. 5:18)

EXCERPT FROM *HEAVEN IS NOW*

Awakening Your Five Spiritual Senses to the Wonders of Grace

by Andrew Farley

In 1998, my father was in a bad car accident. As he lay there in a coma in Fairfax County Hospital, a pastor arrived and tried to heal him. The pastor anointed him with oil, prayed for him, and tried to raise him from the dead. But my dad wouldn't have it. His limp body just lay there, lifeless.

Sometimes we want to change our circumstances. We want to manipulate the externals so that we can somehow feel better on the inside. We want to ask, even in Jesus's name, that things be different.

We want control.

But if you've lived more than a day, you've already figured out that it's not happening. We are *not* in control. Things happen, and we have no say in the matter. Clearly, we're not going to experience something different by controlling our circumstances. Hope must come from somewhere else. Hope must come from heaven *in the midst of* what earth presents us.

Any other hope is delusion.

Invited to Heaven

An early church writer spoke of this hope from heaven: "We have this hope as an anchor for the soul, firm and secure. It enters the inner sanctuary behind the curtain, where our forerunner, Jesus, has entered on our behalf" (Heb. 6:19–20). But Jesus never entered any inner sanctuary in the Jewish temple. He wasn't permitted behind the curtain. Here, the writer means *heaven itself*, where Jesus entered after his resurrection.

But there's more. Speaking of this heavenly sanctuary, the writer then claims that "*we* have confidence to enter the Most Holy Place by the blood of Jesus, by a new and living way" (Heb. 10:19–20). This too means heaven, but this time *we* are invited.

This invitation is not merely about a future in heaven. It's about awakening to a very present hope. Our God has set it up for today, and he invites us to enter in. Why does he bother with such a spectacular invitation?

Because heaven is *now*.

The Kingdom Within

Heaven is *now*?

We're told that God "seated us with him in the heavenly realms" (Eph. 2:6), that "our citizenship is in heaven" (Phil. 3:20), and that we are "aliens and strangers" in this world (1 Pet. 2:11 NASB). We explain these away the best we can. We can't have our faith involving such ridiculous notions. After all, how can any of it really be true here and now in the midst of so much ugliness all around us?

The early church knew this ugliness. They saw it up close and personal as many of them were taken from their families, imprisoned, tortured, even killed. They were no strangers to trouble. Still, they insisted—heaven is *now*.

No, we can't know *all* of heaven here and now. It will take a lifetime and more to gather it in. But even if we only partially realize heaven's splendor on this side, it is still the sweetest form of life to embrace in the midst of all that earth throws our way.

I'm not making any promises that your circumstances will get better. Our circumstances are externals. This book is about what goes on *inside* of us in the midst of our circumstances, not outside or all around us. As Jesus put it, "The kingdom of God is *within* you" (Luke 17:21 NKJV).

Toward the Sky

We hear that heaven is now, and we wish to *feel* it. But our feelings come and go, as we travel from the heights of happiness to the depths of despair in seconds. We ride the roller coaster of the soul every day. So what if the real hope we have is not found in our feelings? Would that kind of hope be worth pursuing?

The way called faith brings this hope from heaven. We have the faith. We need only point it toward the sky. Let me tell you about someone who did.

Horatio Spafford was a wealthy lawyer in Chicago. You could look down a Chicago street and it was nearly all his. Horatio had millions. He also had a lovely wife and four beautiful daughters.

One day, a fire swept through Chicago, destroying nearly all Horatio owned. Two years later he sent his family on vacation across the ocean to England. But their ship went down, and only Horatio's wife survived. He received a telegram from her that read "Saved alone."

Horatio then sailed to England to meet up with his wife, so they could grieve together. On his way, he sat in the hull of that ship and wrote the song, "It Is Well with My Soul."

Horatio lost almost everything. He lost his four daughters and his fortune. His life had turned into tragedy. How could he write that it was well with him? Was he delusional?

As the lyrics of his song reveal, the condition of his soul didn't reflect the circumstances around him. His wellness came as he angled his soul toward heaven. He was awakened to heaven's love. He was reflecting heaven's life. He perceived these with spiritual senses, despite what his physical senses were telling him.

Our Five Spiritual Senses

So how exactly do we experience heaven here and now? We already possess the senses we need to take in heaven's goodness (Heb. 5:14 NASB). We need only have these senses awakened:

- We can *feel* the freedom of God's grace.
- We can *hear* the Spirit bearing witness.
- We can *see* the finished work of Jesus.
- We can *smell* the fragrant aroma of Christ.
- We can *taste* the goodness of the Lord.

Through these five spiritual senses, we experience heaven on this side. We don't see heaven with the natural eye. But by faith we enter into all that it means to be raised and seated with Christ (Eph. 2:6), and we are awakened to heaven's grace.

In preparation for writing this book, I spent many months reading through God's Word, over and over, to take in the big picture. All the while, I was asking: What is heaven trying to tell us?

Here is our first message from heaven.

HEAVEN SPEAKS

My heart's desire is that you rest in me. The heavenly promises I have made to you are designed to give you peace, even in the most violent of storms.

Sometimes you plead with me for a circumstance to change. You ask again and again that it be taken away. My heart longs for you to see more fully how my grace is sufficient for you, even in this. For my power is made perfect in the midst of your weakness.

Through my finished work, I have made you clean and close to me, and you are invited to live in a spiritual seventh day, relaxing in me. But to rest in me takes work. It's not the kind of work you're used to but a very different kind of work. I'm asking you to dig deeper into all that I've done for you so that you can more fully celebrate it, even when outwardly there seems only cause for pain.

I long for you to awaken to the goodness of my grace. As you discover the heights and depths of my love for you, you will experience relationship with me like you never imagined possible.

I love you, and I long for you to know me as I truly am.

Jesus

Awakening TO HEAVEN

Thank you, Jesus, for inviting me to rest. I welcome the adventure of awakening to your grace. I acknowledge that I have no real strength within myself. Instead, I am here, transparent before you, glorying in my weaknesses so that your power may rest on me. I love you, Jesus. And

I want to learn more of your goodness toward me so that you can be my anchor, my stability in any storm.

Heaven Speaks inspired by Hebrews 3:15; 4:9–11; 6:19; John 14:27; 16:33; 2 Corinthians 12:8–10; Ephesians 3:18.

ACKNOWLEDGMENTS

First and foremost, we want to thank our families for their support during our work on this book. A special thank-you goes to Scott Brickell at Brickhouse Entertainment, Andrea Heinecke at Alive Communications, and Lynn Morrow at Adams and Reese LLP for their efforts throughout the process. Additional thanks go to Nate Farro and Brody Harper for their creative design of the album cover art and to Fair Trade Services for granting us permission to use it for the book. We also want to express our gratitude to Baker Publishing Group for partnering with us on the release of this book. In particular, we want to acknowledge Robert Hosack, Wendy Wetzel, Ruth Anderson, Paula Gibson, Brianna DeWitt, and Erin Bartels for their hard work. Lastly, we want to thank you, the reader. If God used this book in your life, we would love to hear from you.

Bart Millard is lead singer for the Christian band MercyMe. Bart was honored as Songwriter of the Year by the Gospel Music Association for "I Can Only Imagine," penned after Bart's father died of cancer. This song rocketed up the charts in 2001 and stayed there as the year's bestselling debut in the Christian music industry. MercyMe's latest album, *The Hurt & The Healer*, hit the Top 10 on iTunes immediately upon release, and the song "The Hurt & The Healer" is the inspiration for this book. Connect with Bart on Twitter (@BartMillard) and visit the MercyMe website (MercyMe.org) to read blogs, watch music videos, and find out more about Bart's tour appearances.

Andrew Farley is lead pastor of Ecclesia (ChurchWithoutReligion.com), a nondenominational Bible church that resides on the high plains of West Texas. Andrew is also the bestselling author of several Christian books including *The Naked Gospel*, *God without Religion*, and *Heaven Is Now*. Andrew's writings have been featured in national news outlets such as PBS, ABC, and FOX. You can hear *Andrew Farley LIVE*, a nationwide call-in program, every Sunday afternoon on Sirius XM Radio. Connect with Andrew on Facebook and Twitter (@DrAndrewFarley), and visit AndrewFarley.org to find out more about his bestselling books.

Heaven Is Now

What if heaven can be enjoyed here on earth RIGHT NOW?

In this life-changing book, bestselling author Andrew Farley reveals how you can take in the beauty of heaven no matter what your circumstances. With insight firmly rooted in the reality of pain and suffering, Andrew assures you that heaven is not merely some pie-in-the-sky dream for the future—it is *now*. He shows you how to awaken your five spiritual senses in order to see, hear, smell, taste, and feel the grace of heaven, even in the midst of trouble here on earth.

Available now!